Meeting the Needs of Student Users in Academic Libraries

CHANDOS
INFORMATION PROFESSIONAL SERIES

Series Editor: Ruth Rikowski
(Email: Rikowskigr@aol.com)

Chandos' new series of books is aimed at the busy information professional. They have been specially commissioned to provide the reader with an authoritative view of current thinking. They are designed to provide easy-to-read and (most importantly) practical coverage of topics that are of interest to librarians and other information professionals. If you would like a full listing of current and forthcoming titles, please visit our website, www.chandospublishing.com, email wp@woodheadpublishing.com or telephone +44(0) 1223 499140.

New authors: we are always pleased to receive ideas for new titles; if you would like to write a book for Chandos, please contact Dr Glyn Jones on gjones@chandospublishing.com or telephone +44 (0) 1993 848726.

Bulk orders: some organisations buy a number of copies of our books. If you are interested in doing this, we would be pleased to discuss a discount. Please email wp@woodheadpublishing.com or telephone +44(0) 1223 499140.

Meeting the Needs of Student Users in Academic Libraries

Reaching across the great divide

MICHELE J. CRUMP AND
LEILANI S. FREUND

WITH CONTRIBUTIONS FROM
STEVEN CARRICO, ANN LINDELL,
PASCAL LUPIEN AND RANDY OLDHAM

CP

CHANDOS
PUBLISHING

Oxford Cambridge New Delhi

Chandos Publishing
Hexagon House
Avenue 4
Station Lane
Witney
Oxford OX28 4BN
UK
Tel: +44 (0) 1993 848726
Email: info@chandospublishing.com
www.chandospublishing.com
www.chandospublishingonline.com

Chandos Publishing is an imprint of Woodhead Publishing Limited

Woodhead Publishing Limited
80 High Street
Sawston
Cambridge CB22 3HJ
UK
Tel: +44 (0) 1223 499140
Fax: +44 (0) 1223 832819
www.woodheadpublishing.com

First published in 2012

ISBN: 978-1-84334-684-5 (print)
ISBN: 978-1-78063-323-7 (online)

British Library Cataloguing-in-Publication Data.
A catalogue record for this book is available from the British Library.

Typeset by Domex e-Data Pvt. Ltd., India
Printed in the UK and USA.

To the memory of our parents:

– Genevieve and Richard Crump – thank you for your love,
the words and music.
– AnnaMae Oliver, who cherished her books – she is always
in the words I write.

Contents

List of figures and tables

Figures

Tables

Acknowledgements

A debt of gratitude is due to all the folks who helped us with our project, we thank you for your creativity and energy: Jami Beserock crunched the data and created all the spreadsheets and graphs – you rock, Jami! Tom Minton "Monkey Man" and Mathew Daley were endlessly patient and are SurveyMonkey™ experts extraordinaire! Brett Diaz, for distributing the survey and chocolate – the evening customers are lucky to have you there. Patrick Reakes and Rachel Schipper – we can't thank you enough for your understanding and encouragement.

Thank you to our contributors for their insight and vision: Steven Carrico and Ann Lindell from the University of Florida and Pascal Lupien and Randy Oldham from the University of Guelph. Thank you to the kind staff of Chandos Publishing for your guidance, and much gratitude especially to Jonathan Davis, who has been with us from the start. Many thanks as well to Sarah Price, who took us to the end.

A special thank you goes to our survey participants for conducting our surveys at their institutions. Without their partnership and the participation of their students and staff, the University of Florida project would have been incomplete. At Oregon State University, Valley Library: Victoria Heiduschke, Learning Commons Coordinator, and Jennifer Nutefall, Associate University Librarian for Innovative User Services. At Syracuse University, E.S. Bird Library: Lisa Moeckel, Associate Dean for Undergraduate Education, Lesley Pease, Head of the Learning Commons, and Nancy Turner, Research & Assessment Analyst. At the University of California, Santa Cruz, McHenry Library, and the Science & Engineering Library: Greg Careaga, Head of Research, Outreach, and Instruction and Lee Jaffe, Planning & Assessment Librarian. At the University of Texas at San Antonio, John Peace Library: Carolyn Cunningham, User Experience Librarian.

To the brilliant librarians and library staff we have worked with through the years – you know who you are and we thank you for your example and guidance.

Michele wishes to thank her family, especially her sister Kimberly, for the encouragement, support and love. Michele also thanks Claire and John Dimsdale for their life-long friendship and through happy circumstances (the wedding of Taylor and Alex) introducing me to Hamish McRae whose book gave our book direction.

LeiLani thanks her Dad, Warren Oliver, for all his encouragement, now and through the years (now you have to read the book, Dad), and to Sheila Oliver, thank you for being my reader and cheerleader. Finally, LeiLani is, as always, thankful to her husband, John, for his patience and understanding and his belief in me – and all the great meals and mighty fine cocktails were essential, too. We couldn't have done this without you, John!

About the authors and contributors

Michele Crump is currently the head of Access Support at the University of Florida Libraries and has responsibility for coordinating circulation policies, processes, and project management for interlibrary loan, document delivery, and electronic course reserves for the libraries. Prior to her current position, she has served in various technical services positions at Florida since 1991: Emerging Technology Librarian, interim Director of Technical Services Division, and Chair of the Acquisitions and Licensing Department. Most recently, she has focused on user-centered services such as unmediated interlibrary loans with the other Florida State University System Libraries; serving on the Emerging Technologies Advisory Group at the University of Florida libraries; and participating in the OLE (Kuali Open Library Environment) project as a member of the Users Stories Teams of the OLE Functional Council.

Michele Crump can be contacted at: *mcrump@ufl.edu*

LeiLani Freund is currently a reference librarian and the linguistics selector and subject specialist at the Library West Humanities and Social Sciences Library, the largest branch of the University of Florida Libraries. She has been at Florida since 1989, serving in a number of managerial positions including a recent term as the interim Chair of Library West following two years as Associate Chair. Other assignments have included Chair of the Humanities and Social Sciences Reference Services Department, Electronic Resources Coordinator, and Head of Interlibrary Loan. As a co-chair and participant in the renovation and redesign of the Library West Humanities and Social Sciences Library in 2006, LeiLani played a leading role in the collaborative effort to establish the first Information Commons in the University of Florida Libraries system.

LeiLani Freund can be contacted at: *leilanif@ufl.edu*

About the contributors

Steven Carrico has been an academic librarian working at the University of Florida since 1994, becoming Chair of the Acquisitions Department in 2006. He has presented at several library conferences and authored or co-authored a wide range of refereed and non-refereed journal articles, published two monograph chapters (in ALA Editions and Haworth Press), book reviews, bibliographies, and was a contributing editor for an Association of Research Libraries (ARL) SPEC kit. Steven has served on numerous national and state library committees, is a columnist for *Against the Grain* and serves on the editorial board for *Library Resources & Technical Services*.

Ann Lindell is Head of the University of Florida Architecture & Fine Arts Library, and serves as Chair of Departmental Libraries. In addition to an MLIS (Master of Library and Information Science) from the University of South Carolina, she holds a BA in Art from Agnes Scott College and an MFA (Master of Fine Arts) in Ceramics from Washington University. She has held leadership positions in several professional organizations including the American Library Association, the Art Libraries Society of North America, and the Association of Architecture School Librarians. Her current research interests deal with the needs of discipline-based branch libraries and with analysis of trends in scholarship by graduate students in the design disciplines.

Pascal Lupien is a Research and Scholarly Communication Librarian at the University of Guelph in Ontario, Canada. He received his MIS (Master of Information Science) from the Université de Montréal in 2001, his MA in Latin American and Caribbean Studies from the University of Guelph in 2009, and is currently working on a PhD. His research interests include the development and evaluation of emerging services, developing services for traditionally underrepresented groups, and understanding how oppressed and powerless groups use information to pursue collective goals.

Randy Oldham is the Web Development Librarian at the University of Guelph. He received his MLIS from the University of Western Ontario in 2009. Randy is currently working towards completing an MA in Leadership at the University of Guelph. Randy manages the web development team, and sits on the user experience team, which is dedicated to ensuring user-friendly experiences to both physical and electronic spaces within the library. Randy has a keen interest in user experience, usage statistics, user behaviors, and student use of technology for learning.

The divide as we see it

Michele J. Crump and LeiLani S. Freund

Abstract: The book is aimed at academic librarians and administrators primarily but will be applicable to all levels of library staff and library and information science students. The introduction is a white paper on what the authors' assumptions are about librarians and library users. The authors work from the following premises: libraries are moving to the digital model; the traditional library catalog is dead; mobility is king; students should be able to access the information anywhere. In the context of this environment, libraries need to look to the user-centric movement and beyond to guide our progress forward.

Key words: information commons (IC), learning commons, librarian perceptions, librarian survey, student perceptions, user experience, user survey.

"It's gone away in yesterday

Now I find myself on the mountainside

Where the rivers change direction

Across the Great Divide"

– K. Wolf (1980) *Across the Great Divide*

Introduction

We have opened our doors for service and they are coming in! We have full-service working computers, emerging technologies to try, printers for class assignments, media software for projects, comfortable chairs, and lattés too. Library gate counts are on the rise as students lounge in the ambience of renovated or brand new spaces that librarians have named information or learning commons.[1] Librarians at the reference desk see students collaborating with other students, communicating with their instructors by email or online course software, and even calling their parents, yet completely bypassing the reference librarian who stands ready to facilitate the research process and point the way to free, reliable library resources. Are we or are we not a part of the collective academic process? Library statistical reports and surveys muddy the waters, often conflicting with one another or with our local results. What are we to believe, what should guide our progress forward?

The 2010 Online Computer Library Center (OCLC) survey *Perceptions of Libraries: Context and Community* makes us feel better with its report that "Library use is the lifestyle activity with the largest increase for all Americans" (De Rosa et al., 2011, p. 26) This is particularly true of the economically vulnerable. However, our confusion returns when we read further that 78 percent of the college students surveyed believe that the librarian adds value to the search process but they overwhelmingly (82 percent) use search engines like Google and Wikipedia to start their research. All the library activities that students engage in are down from a very similar OCLC 2005 survey. For example, using online databases is down 13 percent and using assistance for research is down 20 percent even though 65 percent of students acknowledge that Wikipedia is less trustworthy than library sources. Moreover, library researchers have reported that the Association of Research Libraries (ARL) statistics show a steady decline in reference questions asked from 1991 to the present. Many, though not all, individual library case studies have cited similar figures. The OCLC study gives us some interesting facts about virtual library resources as well. In 2005, only 1 percent of all participants surveyed (that is all ages and all types of library users) visited their library's website first when starting their research. In 2010, *not a single person* out of the 2229 respondents began their information search on a library website (De Rosa et al., 2011, p. 32). Academic students in particular eventually made their way to the website or were told to go there and some said they would go back to it, but not one started there. This statistic should make librarians think very hard about the design of our home pages or portals to online library resources and where we are placing our efforts.

We hoped that the information commons (IC) would revitalize our libraries and indeed they have, in many ways. Libraries frequently report a significant and sometimes astonishing upturn in gate counts after establishment of an IC. We know that the students love our spaces and that the "library as place" is alive and filled with a renewed energy that is palpable. So why is the library journal literature rife with articles that express our insecurity with our role in the digital world?

There are probably as many IC configurations as there are libraries, but they all share the common theme of providing resources that support the users' needs from start to finish of their academic projects and papers. With the advent of the IC, libraries moved from providing and storing the information to providing access and assistance in the gathering, organization, and packaging of information. Needless to say, this has resulted in a profound effect on the library staff operating in this multi-dimensional and highly technical environment and has also called into question services that have existed for several decades. It is no wonder that librarians who have been in the business for 20 or 30 or even as little as 10 years are feeling uncomfortable. In the context of the IC we begin to think about how much our users need or want us to be there. When questions do come in, they are often of a routine directional or technical nature. The directional questions could be answered by a student assistant or volunteer. The technical questions can be downright scary. It's reassuring to read the OCLC report that tells us we are trusted and valued and especially needed in trying economic times, but for every comforting statistic, we see several others that directly contradict the notion that we have a purpose and instead scream our obsolescence. How comforting is it to pick up a copy of *USA Today* and read a headline that blurts out the bad news (as if we didn't know) "Study: College students rarely use librarians' expertise"? (Kolowich, 2011). To add insult to injury, we can read the *whole paper*, because we have plenty of time to read while sitting at the reference desk on the lonely 10 am shift! What is going on here? If they trust us so much, why aren't they lining up at the desk?

One of the inspirations for this book comes from the intriguing and insightful book by Hamish McRae (2010) entitled *What Works: Success in Stressful Times*. McRae is a leading European futurist, economist, and associate editor of *The Independent*. A commentator on Google and other search engines, he has addressed library audiences such as the Research Libraries Group. McRae's book looks at organizations and communities that simply work. As he notes in the introduction to his book, "It is about success in good times and bad" (McRae, 2010, p. ix). After looking at a number of case studies as diverse as Harvard University, IKEA, and the Edinburgh Festival, McRae lists ten lessons to be drawn from these success stories.[2] He goes on to say that to work really well, organizations absolutely need to combine the final two lessons in his list: (1) Having a deep-seated sense of mission; and (2) Being acutely sensitive to the market:

One without the other does not work. A plan or project that operates with a mission but fails to listen to the market may carry on for a while on a tide of early enthusiasm. But it cannot be sustained. Pure market-driven endeavours can carry on for much longer ... But add the sense of mission and you get something much more: a success that can be replicated and scaled. (McRae, 2010, pp. xi–xii)

In the context of the modern library/IC and the economic realities of the recession and the twenty-first century, librarians need more than ever to look at "what works" in our libraries and remove the legacy services that do not. In this spirit, the authors have made a few assumptions about the direction libraries need to take to more proactively meet users' needs and maintain vital services. The reader may not agree with these assumptions and indeed we may ruffle more than a few feathers, but without a candid discussion of what does not work, we cannot have a meaningful discussion of what does. Our assumptions include the following:

- Librarians make assumptions about what students need, but often without asking them. One of the key mistakes we make is generalizing; for example, characterizing the Millennials as digital natives and ignoring the gaps in their comfort level with the technology and information science.

- The Internet has created an environment in which our users expect information on their own terms, anywhere and anytime. Libraries must compete with other information providers to deliver this level of service.

- As of this moment, the patron still needs librarians but often does not know it and this need lessens with each passing day. We should not delude ourselves; the likelihood of becoming irrelevant is real.

- The library catalog in the traditional sense is dead. Adding more features to it or creating a web-like overlay does not revive it. Libraries need to work with library software developers to enhance true discoverability.

- The library website is on life support.

- Mobile technology is key, but maybe not quite as we expected. The smartphone may not have the utility we thought it would for library services, but other mobile technology will. The future is in mobility.

- Most libraries are undergoing serious to severe budget cuts and it is unlikely for the foreseeable future that this will change. Librarians need to accept this and deal with it.

- Academic libraries will be held accountable for expenditures to a greater degree and expected to contribute to learning outcomes.

- Libraries are moving toward the digital model and print circulation is down. Print collections will continue to exist but will likely be concentrated in certain subject areas or in special collections; lower use print titles will be located off-site and in shared storage areas.

- The academic library as place is a valid assumption supported by gate counts.

- The establishment of information and learning commons increases usage of the building but not necessarily of services like research assistance.

- Academic libraries are moving too slowly. We think we know where we want to go but we get bogged down in committees and bureaucratic structure. We need to do whatever it takes organizationally and individually to be adaptable.

The above statements set the stage for what the authors believe are realities that substantiate the great divide between the librarian's desire to serve and the student's need for applicable library service. More to the point, librarians want to know if they are still relevant in the academic community. The authors agree with some visionary leaders in the profession that libraries have upheld legacy services and processes "that are ignored or undervalued by their clients" (Michalko, 2010, p. 19) to the detriment of users' immediate or future needs. To take that thinking a little further, we believe that librarians continue such services because of the comfort factor and the belief that these services are filling a customer need. Juxtaposing this position, librarians have adopted innovative services in the rush to take the library to the cutting edge. However, adopting new services and tools, "can create as many problems as they solve, and it is critical to be as conscious of a local context as possible during the planning process" (Booth, 2009, p. 140). Often these services have not been well received or even adopted by users because we have not involved them in any usability consulting or marketing trials before or after implementing a new resource or service. Asking students to try new products and receiving their useful feedback will help us make far-thinking, sustainable decisions that should contribute lasting value to the library users' experience.

Academic libraries are delighting their customers with renovated spaces that are more compatible with students' study habits. Now it is time that libraries delight their clientele with services that evoke a pleasant remembered experience as we fully support their academic endeavors. User-centered, self-service, or patron-driven services, no matter how the concept is labeled, signify a library movement in which the customer is asked to engage in library decision making. For example, at the University of Florida the "Books on Demand" program gives patrons the opportunity to ask that a book be purchased if the library does not have it in the collection.[3] Why is this program so popular and working well? The customer offers explicit input, the library purchases the resource, and in a matter of days the item is in the patron's hands – that is a positive user experience! This beneficial model contains a "Wow!" element that Stephen Bell (2010) praises as key to successful user experience, aptly pointing out that "as more organizations design better experiences for consumers, to retain their customers and attract new ones it is essential to imagine and implement new and better experiences that are unexpected and remarkable"(p. 112).

If delighting our customers and closing the divide are goals, librarians need to step-up the pace, quit floundering, and start building sustainable relationships with the faculty and students we so want to serve. Why does it often take librarians so long to find a solution, tweak the solution to meet library needs, live with it until it is no longer useful, and finally move on to the next solution? We give lip service to abandoning traditional services and workflows but in reality we cling to these practices. Instead, we should be stepping from behind the desk as so many enlightened librarians have proposed and initiating conversations with our customers, particularly when they are not coming to the desk to talk with us. Let us start by asking our customers to help us identify service issues and inviting them to be part of the problem-solving process; engage them in the process of building a plan that will further revitalize the library as place. Such action could be the beginning of fostering that sense of community and responsibility necessary for keeping library services germane to students, faculty, and the library staff.

Paraprofessionals and student employees play a significant role in the service face of the library and are in fact usually the staff patrons have the most contact with when they do approach a service desk. We have long been aware that patrons do not distinguish between librarians and paraprofessionals. In fact, recent studies show that students do not think that library employees on the whole can help them with their academic projects. (Foster & Gibbons, 2007) We have not done much in academic libraries to change patrons' perceptions. To encourage user-centered service, library organizations will need to institute more development training that addresses library staff members and their sensitivity to the customer's experience, particularly in the area of putting themselves in the place of the customer. Bivens-Tatum (2010) expresses the obvious succinctly: "It's a matter of moral reasoning as much as anything else. Imagination and sympathy. What would we want if we were in the place of the user?"

The authors suspect that library staff working on the more service-centric desks such as circulation may be experiencing burnout not only from customer overload but from the additional burden of keeping pace with new technology plus performing legacy services. Even though burnout is not a new problem it does seem to be a persistent one in the library world. We encourage libraries to consider new desk staffing models and rotations that give library staff "sabbaticals" from desk service. We also urge library managers to institute competency training for all staff levels in evolving technologies and routinely offer continuing education classes on new resources. Such commitment to skill enhancement will build confidence while helping staff meet the technological expectations of library users. Like the customer, all library staff members need to be valued for their creativity and individual talents. Nurturing employees on the job will only benefit the image of the library – confident and happy staff adds to the welcoming factor rooted in library as place.

Librarians and paraprofessionals are embarking on a new era of user experience and ethnographic studies that attempt to truly define our customers' behavior. With these revitalizing movements, we have an opportunity to connect our services with student needs and measure learning outcomes as we never have before. To that end, we need to be responsive, timely, open-minded, and above all agile. Will librarians be able to use the findings reported here to advise the evolution and implementation of new service models or will we simply put a different shade of lipstick on the pig? The following chapters show that librarians are acting to realize answers – they envision a better pig. The authors are encouraged by the user-centered focus in the studies we have included here and feel optimistic that the profession will be able to redefine its raison d'être.

Book layout

The above white paper outlines the authors' assumptions about librarians and library users. In that context, we examine IC development in academic libraries and evaluate whether it fulfills the promise of being a central place where students may collaborate while having access to a variety of technology that will support their research. The authors worked from a number of premises that include the following: libraries are moving to the digital model; the traditional library catalog is dead; mobility is king; students expect to access resources anytime from anywhere.

Following this introduction, Chapter 2 by LeiLani Freund considers current service models in IC/learning commons through pertinent writings, visits, and surveys that evaluate what is working and what is not. She highlights academic libraries that demonstrate innovative and sustainable approaches to service issues and those that invite further exploration. The chapter closes with a discussion of the fate of the reference desk in the commons environment. Steven Carrico and Ann Lindell in Chapter 3 address the physical design of the IC profiling several academic libraries that have renovated or constructed exceptional collaborative spaces. They evaluate how these new spaces address the academic and technological needs of students on these campuses. In Chapter 4 Michele Crump reviews library assessment practices focusing on recent anthropological studies that define the student population in a real way. She considers case studies that demonstrate the user experience model and reveals how it is building customer relationships in academic libraries. Chapter 5 offers a detailed analysis by Pascal Lupien and Randy Oldham of the 2007 and 2010 surveys they conducted at the University of Guelph in Ontario, Canada to evaluate students' use of technology. Their survey results offer insight about the types of technology students are utilizing the most and applying to their studies in the academic environment. In Chapter 6 Michele Crump and LeiLani Freund discuss the methodology and development of the two survey instruments they designed to gage library user and staff perceptions. They report the individual and combined results from the academic libraries that participated in the study: University of Florida; Syracuse University; Oregon State University; University of Texas at San Antonio; University of California, Santa Cruz. The authors analyze and compare the two survey responses to measure the "divide" between user and librarian perceptions about library as place and library as resource/service provider. In Chapter 7 Crump and Freund use their survey findings to examine the dynamics between students and librarians and between librarians and administrators. The apparent miscommunication revealed in their research seems to be systemic throughout the library profession – unfortunately this is not news. However, there are also similarities in the perceptions of students and librarians and these are what we need to build on and take action. The authors will address the issues and look to the user-centric movement and beyond to find far-thinking answers that may guide us to the future. Appendices A and B include the internal survey instruments the above authors conducted to test their research assumptions.

Notes

1. The terminology for the "information commons" or "learning commons" is somewhat variable in usage and will be discussed more fully in Chapter 2. For purposes of this introduction, the authors define the information commons in a similar way to the definition used by Beagle in *The Information Commons Handbook*: "a new type of physical facility or section of a library specifically designed to organize workspace and service delivery around an integrated digital environment and the technology that supports it" (Beagle, 2006, p. 3). We generally use the term "learning commons" to denote the evolution of the commons to an even more collaborative environment that involves campus entities outside the library to support the whole learning process.

2. From "Introduction, I. How this book happened – and how it has changed during the writing", The Lessons: "1. Optimism, balanced by realism; pessimism paralyses. 2. Excellence, tempered by decency: if you neglect your wider responsibilities, you're liable to end up in trouble when you meet headwinds. 3. Community works, if it is allowed to: look at things from the ground level up and mobilize community. 4. Government works too: compare like with like. 5. Become a true magnet for talent: put out the welcome mat. 6. Be honest about failure: keep learning, keep making mistakes. 7. The need for humility: be as sensitive to success as you are to failure. 8. Be nimble: make sure you are quick to adapt. 9. Listen to the market: remember, it's about more than money. 10. Have a sense of mission: keep the long game in view and do right by those who share your objectives" (McRae, 2010, p. x).

3. See Foss (2007) for more information on the Books-on-Demand program at University of Florida Libraries.

References

Beagle, D. R. (2006). *The information commons handbook*. New York: Neal-Schuman Publishers.

Bell, S. (2011, 13 July). Keeping the antennae up: How listening in the library improves UX. *Designing Better Libraries*. Retrieved from *http://dbl.lishost.org/blog/2011/07/13/keeping-the-antennae-up-how-listening-in-the-library-improves-ux*

Bivens-Tatum, W. (2010, 15 November). Imagination, sympathy, and the user experience. *Library Journal, 19*. Retrieved from *http://www.libraryjournal.com/lj/reviewsreference/887365-283/imagination_sympathy_and_the_user.html.csp*

Booth, C. (2009). *Informing innovation: Tracking student interest in emerging library technologies at Ohio University*. Chicago: Association of College & Research Libraries.

De Rosa, C., Cantrell, J., Carlson, M., Gallagher, M., Hawk, J., Sturtz, C., et al. (2011). *Perceptions of libraries: Context and community*. Dublin, OH: OCLC Online Computer Library Center, Inc. Retrieved from *http://www.oclc.org.reports/2010perceptions/2010perceptions_all.pdf*

Foss, M. (2007). Books-on-demand pilot program: An innovative patron-centric approach to enhance the library collection. *Journal of Access Services, 5*(1), 305–315.

Foster, N. F., & Gibbons, S. (2007). *Studying Students: The Undergraduate Research Project at the University of Rochester*. Chicago: Association of College and Research Libraries.

Kolowich, S. (2011, 22 August). Study: College students rarely use librarians' expertise. *USA Today*. Retrieved from *http://www.usatoday.com/news/education/2011-08-22-college-students-librarians_n.htm*

McRae, H. (2010). *What works: Success in stressful times*. London: Harper Press.

Michalko, J., Malpas, C., & Arcolio, A. (2010). *Research libraries, risk and systematic change*. Dublin, OH: OCLC Research. Retrieved from *http://www.oclc.org/research/publications/library/2010/2010-03.pdf*

Wolf, K. (1980). *Across the great divide*. Forest Knolls, CA: Another Sundown Publishing.

2

Services in the information commons

LeiLani S. Freund

Abstract: The information commons has become a key component of the public services offerings in most academic libraries. This chapter provides a short background and definition of the information commons concept in its current evolving state. Snapshots are provided of successful library commons service models that convey a mission or directive that will sustain their usefulness and not simply tolerate change, but exemplify change to fit the needs of their customers; in short, these information/learning commons "work." The chapter will conclude with a discussion of an issue that persists in library public services and especially in the information commons context: "Is the reference desk dead?"

Key words: academic libraries, chat reference, information commons (IC), information technology (IT), knowledge commons, learning commons, mobile technologies, research assistance, reference, roving reference.

"The overall goal of information commons is to improve services to the campus community by offering a seamless environment that supports the way people work."

– J. K. Lippincott (2006). Linking the information commons to learning, p. 74

"In ten years, will there still be an academic reference desk? There will be, because I know how hard it is for an academic library to get rid of a piece of furniture."

– M.L. Radford (2011). *A future in transition: Foreseeing forthcoming opportunities & challenges in academic reference*

Introduction

The concept of the information commons (IC) has dominated much of the discussion of public services in libraries for the last 20 years. A substantial portion of the library literature has documented the evolution of this now ubiquitous and attention-grabbing centerpiece of library services. In this chapter, the author will survey some of the literature and discuss service issues that arise in the commons environment as well as featuring successful examples from the standpoint of service, innovation, and both the flexibility and sustainability to develop as a true partner in the education process. It is not the purpose of this chapter to provide a comprehensive review of all the literature on the information and learning commons. Excellent case studies, overviews, and bibliographies cover the prolific writing on this subject (see "References" and "Additional Resources" at the end of the chapter.) Some of the highlighted articles in this chapter represent important benchmarks in the development of the IC; others describe thoughtful approaches to the service issues; and some simply intrigue and invite further exploration. The chapter that follows, from two University of Florida colleagues, will more thoroughly discuss the information commons facility in the physical sense.

Background

In January 2012, an interesting discussion took place on the INFOCOMMONS-L listserv after one list member asked when the information commons and learning commons models first appeared in the academic literature. Donald Beagle, academic library director and well-known consultant in this subject area, replied that he first heard the term in a talk by Robert Lucky of Bell Labs. Beagle says that in 1987 or 1988 Lucky mentioned libraries as "places where students and the public might soon go to access 'the online information commons'" (Beagle, 2012). However, as early as 1974, a group of representatives from industry leaders such as Bell Labs, General Electric, and Xerox gathered with President Robert Plane of Clarkson University in New York to discuss not a traditional library but a location that would store books or information of any format (Plane, 1982). In 1985, Pat Molholt, the Associate Director of Libraries at Rensselaer Polytechnic Institute predicted in a *Journal of Academic Librarianship* article that libraries and computing centers were on a "converging path" (1985, p. 284). She went on further to say that the systems designers would not have the perspective needed on information-seeking behaviors or on the nature of information itself; librarians would need to provide that perspective. Molholt does not use the phrase "information commons" but clearly had something like the IC concept in mind and she accurately predicted the profound impact of information technology (IT) on librarianship and the need to help library staff to adjust to a new model (Molholt, 1985).

Both the concept and the phrase "information commons" were being used at several locations by the early 1990s, including the University of Iowa, Estrella Mountain Community College, and the University of Southern California's Leavey Library. IC projects grew exponentially over the next ten years. The IC often resided in or replaced what was once the reference area, but sometimes later expanded to an entire floor or comprised an entire renovated library. Sometimes, rather than being placed in a library, the commons was created to be more like a computer lab, existing in a separate building such as the one at the University of Toronto. Donald Beagle, in the *Information Commons Handbook*, notes that the term has been used alongside such labels as Information Arcade, Media Union, and Virtual Village but information commons persisted and continues to be used as "the term most frequently and generically applied" (Beagle, 2006, p. 3). Although wi-fi has changed the network paradigm, the rest of Beagle's definition still holds up: "a cluster of network access points and associated IT tools situated in the context of physical, digital, human, and social resources organized in support of learning" (Beagle, 2006, p. xviii). The underlying philosophy, as Joan Lippincott of the Coalition for Networked Information notes, "is to provide users with a seamless work environment so that they may access, manage, and produce information all at the same workstation" (Lippincott, 2006, p. 7.2).

Increasingly (but not entirely consistently), libraries have turned to the term "learning commons" and "knowledge commons" or "research commons" to stress the extended, collaborative nature of these spaces. The IC has evolved in the twenty-first century to a center of learning and education that draws upon the resources of various campus groups to provide more comprehensive support for the students. The University of Washington Library web page entitled "What is the Research Commons?" (*http://commons.lib.washington.edu/about*) describes the University of Washington facility as a place to connect, providing "a collaborative environment in which students and faculty can come together to share and discuss research, as well as get support for all steps of the research process: searching, writing, publishing, funding" (University of Washington Libraries, n.d.). In *7 Things You Should Know About™ the Modern*

Learning Commons, the reader is reminded of the societal function of the village commons, a gathering place that focused on relationships and social connections (EDUCAUSE Learning Initiative (ELI), 2011).

The extended library commons provides traditional library services along with food and drink, comfortable furniture and lounge areas, individual and group work spaces, computers, and media resources. They are spaces where students, faculty, IT staff, and librarians gather not only to find information, but to create knowledge. How they will further develop will depend on the partnerships forged across campus and the technology on the horizon. The possibilities are endless, so the developers and participating library staff must be flexible and open to new roles, and the design must be flexible to accommodate innovation and change.

What works in the information commons environment

There can be no question that when establishing an IC, or any other technologically rich environment, money (lots of it) helps. Also critically important to the formation of the commons and certainly to the continued success of the venture will be collaboration between units of the library and of the campus overall, a clearly stated vision, and input from students, faculty, and staff. The following examples are not, by any measure, the only successful commons; there are many innovative, service-oriented ICs that attract high praise from their users as well as outsiders. The few that follow are particularly good examples of the service quality and agility the author feels is necessary if libraries are to maintain their viability in the future.

The circle of service: articulating the vision

The most common collaboration is the one between the academic library and the campus computer or IT office. As described in the "Background" section of this chapter, the computer center was very much on the mind of the library directors and university presidents who first began discussing the library as a center of information access. Barbara Dewey, former Dean of Libraries at the University of Tennessee, Knoxville, speaks eloquently of the planning for their IC (which would be called simply "The Commons") and the "Circle of Service" model at the University of Tennessee that has as one of its guiding principles the "true partnership of the Libraries and OIT [Office of Information Technology]" (Dewey, 2008, p. 44). She further envisions the goal to be "slashing bureaucracy and providing uncompromising service in a user-centered environment" (Dewey, 2008, p. 54). This collaborative concept has guided the construction of the impressive Hodges Library Commons at the University of Tennessee, extending to the planning, funding, and implementation of all three phases of the project. Student and faculty advisory groups were also key players at all stages of the process. Phase I of the project opened in 2005, but the OIT and Libraries had embarked on a partnership years before with the development in 2001 of the Digital Media Service (DMS). The Hodges Library effort was such a success that it guided later campus-wide initiatives and became the model for other computer labs on campus. The vision statement is expressed as a partnership "to connect students and faculty with the tools and information they need to be successful learners and teachers in the 21st century" (Dewey and Little, 2006). The OIT maintains a help desk in the IC and the facility is open around the clock Monday through Thursday.

The successful outcome of the University of Tennessee collaboration was measurable from the very beginning. Within one year of the opening, the total gate count was up 46 percent. Circulation of books and equipment was up by 79 percent. After the second phase of the project, as many as 400 students were counted in the Commons at midnight, mid-week (Dewey & Little, 2006). Colleges and other units on campus approached the library soon after the first phase to discuss placing services in the Commons. The University of Tennessee Hodges Commons works because it began with a clear vision and a partnership that has sustained itself so well that its influence has extended across the university.

Leveraging the support of partners in the commons

The importance of the coalition with the IT department clearly emerges from an examination of successful IC initiatives. Sometimes the technical support may come from within the library structure in the form of a library IT office. However, many of the libraries the authors studied are, like the University of Tennessee Hodges Commons, either already working closely with the campus IT office or about to explore such a relationship. In some cases, universities are considering the consolidation of IT departments, a trend that is likely to continue as universities struggle with declining budgets and the need to be cost-effective. Increasingly and especially for the large facilities, the library needs both the expertise and the financial support of the campus IT department.

Joan Lippincott warns that in the new commons environments "Staff of the various units often offer the same types of services they offered prior to the information commons: they do not take advantage of the new configuration to rethink their services or staffing patterns" (Lippincott, 2006, p. 7.11). She notes the innovative staffing at Georgia Tech where "the library and IT units provide intensive multimedia creation training to graduate students who then assist other students in a heavily used space" (Lippincott, 2006, p. 7.11). In another example of reinvention from Lippincott (2006), Dartmouth integrated its library, IT services, and the writing center (*http://www.dartmouth.edu/~rwit/*) in one place, the Berry Library. All three units train tutors to offer peer-to-peer assistance in a full range of services including generation of ideas for papers, research strategies, writing drafts, writing creatively, and creating multimedia projects.

The IC at the University of Calgary Library was one of the earlier IC initiatives, opening in 1999. Right from the start of the project it was determined that the IT unit of the University of Calgary would be an active partner in planning and developing the commons and also in the delivery of ongoing services. IT would also team up with the library in paying for maintenance and replacement of the computers and software (Beatty, 2010). Initially, the plan at the University of Calgary was to have all the reference desk staff trained by the IT unit to assist patrons with technical support. According to Susan Beatty, this training helped to put the staff more at ease with helping users. However, it became apparent very quickly that an expectation of the same level of expertise for every member of the staff was impractical. The IT unit and the library agreed to share the costs of student technical assistants who would help to run the 24-hour facility. These students were later named "Student Navigators" and they became the IT experts. They are hired and maintained as employees not just for their IT skills but for their customer service abilities, self-direction, maturity, and reliability (Beatty, 2010). The Student Navigators have ongoing training with the librarians in basic research skills. The IT unit does all the technical training and supervision. Although there were originally four IT staff in a separate office in the IC, the budget has reduced them to one IT staff member who now has an office with the library staff, the advantage of which is the adjacency of library and IT staff for the critical communication needed in a 24-hour facility (Beatty, 2010). The University of Calgary commons is a success because the library has fostered a working collaboration with the campus IT unit since the inception of the commons. Together they have created an expert team of student peer-assistants chosen for their fit with the goals of established library customer service best practices and, in an era of staff cuts, no doubt invaluable to maintaining good service.

Contrast these examples of realignment of libraries and IT with the older model, still in use at some libraries, where IT support is provided only at the point of need and often through a trouble ticket system of some kind. No matter how responsive and helpful the technical staff may be, there is little opportunity in this organizational model for the librarians to discuss the needs of the students with the technical staff in any meaningful or long-term way. Such support puts out fires but has no sustained plan forward, nor is there any opportunity for the IT staff to view and understand the dynamics of the commons environment. One perceived advantage to this model from the administrative point of view may be that it reinforces the need for library staff on the front-line to keep up with the technology in order to give basic triage tech support, but does this provide service excellence and leverage the skills of the IT staff to its fullest?

The University of Florida (UF) George A. Smathers Libraries is an example of a system that employs the trouble ticket/triage model. The IT office staff is now housed off-site, so the opportunity for skills transfer is rare. Student assistants for the public commons areas are trained by the librarians. In an unpublished study by Marilyn Ochoa and LeiLani Freund, UF staff members were queried four years apart (2005–08) to ascertain comfort with the technology in the IC. Within those five years, little had changed. Librarians and paraprofessionals were fairly comfortable with common software such as Microsoft Office, but not at ease with scanning, multimedia creation, or special software and hardware for students with disabilities. Ochoa and Freund determined that 75 percent of the issues about which staff was concerned were related to restrictive security measures on the public workstations. Although these problems were eventually reconciled, they could have been resolved much sooner with direct observation by the IT specialists. Organizations that fail to leverage the combined talents of appropriate units sustain an internal divide that impedes a quick response. The authors predict that this type of system is too impractical to survive in the current university political and financial environment and in an era of disruptive change. It is a legacy model.

Emerging technologies

Some libraries with their partners are making the IC a centerpiece of new technologies to explore innovations in the creation and packaging of knowledge. The Digital Union at Ohio State University was established in 2004 in the Science and Engineering Library. It brings together the Office of the Chief Information Officer (CIO) on campus and the Libraries. The purpose of the center is to showcase emerging technologies and also to support the students, staff, and faculty who undertake media projects or "exploration of technology in academic environments and in society as a whole" (Getis, Gynn, & Metros, p. 31.1). The Digital Union is unique because it resides in a library, with librarians participating alongside technical support staff and vendors demonstrating new technologies.

The libraries at Ohio State University also received a Library Services & Technology Act (LSTA) Innovative Technology Grant to experiment with Vocera, a Voice-over Internet Protocol (VoIP) system that is popular in the healthcare industry, enabling mobile workers to do hands-free communication using badges and voice recognition capabilities. This kind of system would seem to have enormous potential in larger buildings, enabling, for example, a staff member shelving books to broadcast a call to any available reference librarian to come and help a student who approaches them for assistance. The Vocera project came to an end in January 2011. Sarah Murphy, Coordinator of Research and Reference, said that "use of the technology did not pan out as hoped" but "did help us see that there is value in having a point-of-need communication system for our patrons" (Murphy, 2010: 24 September blog entry).

There has been much discussion of the use of mobile technologies in libraries to expand service options. Staff at the Morris Library at Southern Illinois University-Carbondale (Lotts & Graves, 2011), at the University of Northern British Columbia's Weller Library (MacDonald & McCabe, 2011), and at the University of Florida are experimenting with iPads for reference librarians. Results have been mixed and/or are just getting underway but there is no doubt that tablet technology makes the roving concept much easier to implement. Tablet products will get better and better – the author believes service mobility is the future and it will evolve much beyond texting and the roving librarian models that some libraries have tried.

The D.H. Hill Library of North Carolina State University (NCSU) has a popular loan program for a wide array of equipment: iPads, laptops, projectors, eReaders, GPS units, and OCR pens, to name only a few (see *http://www.lib.ncsu.edu/techlending*). Other libraries have loan programs, but few as diverse as the NCSU array of equipment, and some have suspended loan programs. The University of California Merced Library has recently discontinued its laptop loan program due to budget constraints and the fact that nearly all the students have their own laptops. It's unclear at this point in which direction libraries will take these services, but one thing for certain is that sustainability depends on a steady flow of cash for purchasing and maintaining equipment.

Regardless of what form it takes, we know that the technologies we rely on now will change rapidly and relentlessly. Librarians in the commons have the advantage of mobile communication and other emerging technologies that provide an increasing array of possibilities for provision of library service. To make the right choices, libraries must find the right blend of staff innovation and enthusiasm (just try something!) while keeping the customer's needs and the library's mission firmly in mind.

Keeping the customer as the focus

Few people may be aware that the University of Central Florida is the second largest university in the United States, with a student population over 58 000. A visit to the library and the new Knowledge Commons in late 2010 emphasized to this author that the main library could be much bigger for the large student population. It was a cold day (for Florida) and the end of the busy fall semester, so the library was packed; every chair was filled. More than 200 computers are available but they are often filled to capacity or near capacity and the space for them is a little crowded. The students were working hard, some individually and some talking quietly in groups, absorbed in their projects. The furniture is modular to enable students to create individual nooks or spaces for groups. It came as a pleasant surprise to see that the reference desk was busy. The desk is situated on the entrance (second) floor and set back a bit, but still quite visible. Both librarians at the desk were engaged with a student and other students seemed to be hovering nearby. Off to the side of the medium-sized desk were smaller areas separated with translucent glass panels to provide a quiet consultation area for a librarian and student to work seated together at a computer workstation; at least one of these was busy each time I walked by. The atmosphere was intense and a little noisy, but not unpleasantly so.

While at the library, I heard a lot about the recent renovation of the library to accommodate more computers and a new Knowledge Commons environment. It seemed, from the librarians' reports and from observation, that the students were very pleased with the renovation. With interest, I saw an old fashioned guest book placed near some comfortable chairs. I read several positive comments on the pages, most of them referring to the improvements in the facility.

A few months later I would hear more from Meg Scharf, Associate Director for Public Services at the University of Central Florida Libraries, in her 2011 Association of College and Research Libraries (ACRL) Virtual Pre-Conference address entitled *Listening to Users ... Closing the Feedback Loop: Just Do It!* presented with Lisabeth Chabot, of the Ithaca College Library. One of their points resonated with its pure practicality: the user feedback and evaluation process cannot be too onerous for either the librarians or the users or it simply will not happen (Scharf & Chabot, 2011). Thinking back to the paper form suggestion boxes and the guest books scattered strategically around the library at the University of Central Florida, I realized why they were there. Scharf noted that the University of Central Florida Libraries get more paper suggestions than electronic. The paper forms have a tear-off sheet at the bottom that explains the means of response and also gives the patron some important phone numbers and emails in case they want to follow up. The University of Central Florida uses a home-grown intranet for the database of comments and the responses.

The University of Central Florida librarians make sure that all comments that provide an address for a response are answered in as short a timeframe as possible. The computer and study room online availability maps are direct results of patron suggestions. When possible, the librarians try to respond within 24 hours. Urgent problems such as network or printing outages are addressed immediately. In this way, the library can make sure that the customers who are concerned enough to take the time to write a complaint or comment will be "surprised and delighted" by a speedy response that immediately implies that someone cares. Given the typically short attention span of the busy students, an immediate response is crucial or they "may lose interest and feel as if their opinions do not count" (Scharf & Chabot, 2011).

There are other initiatives that measure the success of the University of Central Florida Libraries and the Knowledge Commons. Since fall semester 2008, the Main Library has been the site of the Campus Connections program that the libraries developed. Mendelsohn (2012) writes of the success of this program, which brings in campus groups on Tuesdays, one at a time, to promote the group's services and inform students. The program has been a tremendous success. A 2011 survey of the campus partners indicated 93 percent were very pleased with the overall program. They described the benefits of the partnership as an opportunity to connect with students in a setting in which they were not in competition with one another for the students' attention and a good means of increasing their visibility. Twenty-four organizations participated in spring 2011, engaging in conversation with 904 students.

Bucking the trend in falling reference statistics, Scharf reported in her presentation that the Main Library at the University of Central Florida has seen an increase in reference desk questions of 77 percent since the Knowledge Commons redesign and they are back to double and triple desk staffing (Scharf & Chabot, 2011). She attributes this in part to the overall increase in traffic since the renovation but also to the renewed efforts to receive and answer user feedback. In addition to the suggestion boxes, they have engaged in numerous informal interviews with the students and have also done some affinity-mapping events in which students group the services most essential to them. The librarians and their partners at the University of Central Florida Knowledge Commons are making it personal and creating an environment that works because it puts the user first.

Reference services: the dinosaur in the commons?

Now that the author has dared to bring up reference statistics in the context of the University of Central Florida Knowledge Commons, this brings us to a legacy service on every public service librarian's mind: the reference desk. The rumor is persistent; like the reference collection, the reference desk seems to be fading fast in the technologically disruptive commons environment.

What the statistics show

The traditional services in academic libraries have manifested themselves in the desk model. For years, the library staff has been strategically placed at a circulation desk that is usually close to the entrance and exit (often for security purposes as well as convenience), providing check-out and return of library materials, help with circulation problems, access to reserves and special items held behind the desk, and general, directional information. Sometimes, an information or triage desk might also be part of the circulation desk area or placed near the entrance for maximum visibility. The reference or research assistance desk was usually near the reference collection and it was and still is often staffed by some combination of public service librarians and well-trained public service paraprofessionals. The librarians are sometimes subject specialists and collection managers as well. Smaller branch libraries might be more likely to combine all circulation, information, and reference functions into one desk. The IC in some libraries displaced or moved into the reference area and brought about a new service point – the IT help desk. This required new partnerships and staffing models, some of which have been discussed in the first part of this chapter.

Certainly, the library IC has significantly changed the dynamics of the librarian–patron interaction. Now all the action centers on the patron's use of the workstations. While students in the past were quietly studying in the library or seeking material, usually at least aware of the librarian at the reference desk, now typical users are totally engaged with their computer and finding much of what they need delivered directly to their desktop. If the service desks and/or signs are not well placed in the sea of IC computers, the student who encounters a problem may be totally unaware of the existence of librarian assistance or may not know where to go for help. Indeed, even the aware person is unlikely to want to log off the computer, gather up valuable belongings and trek to the desk. If students don't worry about the security of their logged on computers or their belongings, they may live to regret their unconcern. There are many other reasons why today's students do not approach the desk; these are explored in the Crump/Freund survey (see Chapter 6).

Statistical surveys and reports, such as Association of Research Libraries (ARL) compilations, have led librarians to the certainty that reference or research assistance activities in academic libraries have undergone a dramatic decrease over the past two decades. Charles Martell (2007) provides a detailed report of changing use patterns at ARL, Association of College and Research Libraries (ACRL), Association of Southeastern Research Libraries (ASERL), and other organizations that shows inconsistencies in circulation statistics but an overall steep decline in reference statistics from 1995 to 2004. Yale showed a drop of 71 percent while other ARL institutions in Martell's list showed only a little less disturbing decreases of 44 percent to 54 percent. (Martell, 2007, p. 442) Marie Radford, professor at Rutgers University and a frequent library conference speaker and organizer of the Reference Renaissance Conferences, cites studies that demonstrate a drop in face-to-face reference accompanied by a steady increase in virtual forms of reference (mainly email and chat.) Along with the increase in chat reference traffic, there seems to be a corresponding complexity to the questions received through the chat medium (Radford, 2008). An examination of University of Florida chat transcripts seems to corroborate the perception of complexity, along with an increase in activity of nearly 25 percent per year over the last three years.

Radford is not convinced, however, that reference statistics overall have dropped quite as much as reported: "I strongly suspect that one reason we are seeing a decrease in the reference statistics for academic libraries is because there is a lag in figuring out how to count reference questions given the increase in online and other nontraditional reference activity" (Radford, 2008, p. 111). In a 2002 ARL SPEC Kit entitled *Reference Service Statistics & Assessment*, the responders gave their libraries poor self-ratings in the collection, analysis, and use of data, indicating "widespread dissatisfaction with current practices relating to reference transactions" Novotny (2002, p. 11) and "a general lack of confidence in current data collection techniques" (p. 12). The software for data collections has improved with programs such as Desk Tracker™ and Springshare's LibAnalytics, which facilitate not only counting but analysis of demographics and duration and complexity of questions. However, the human problem still persists. How well do librarians manage to record statistics for queries that are answered in so many formats and venues and how motivated are they to log into databases to do so? Unfortunately, the busy times at the desk are precisely when the staff is least likely to record.

The real reason we worry

Although statistics do not give us the whole picture, any librarian who has been doing reference for the past 15 years or more will tell you they have experienced dramatic changes. In the late 1990s the reference desk at the University of Florida's Humanities & Social Sciences Library West was very busy. The desk was usually scheduled with two professional librarians and one paraprofessional but there were still lines. The questions were varied and instructors gave class assignments that would require going to the library to look at paper indexes and abstracts, such as finding a folk-tale motif in the Stith-Thompson Motif-Index; looking up book reviews in the Book Review Index, or searching the complicated Citation indexes (Social Sciences Citation Index, etc.). Sometimes we put reference books out on trucks for specific classes. Two things scared me: (1) having to get on the Dialog database (just dialing in was difficult enough, let alone trying to find something with the ridiculous search keys); and (2) business questions. The University of Florida has a large graduate program in business and most of us tried to avoid business questions. Many business resources were on multiple CD-ROMs and had to be used on particular workstations. It was advantageous to be short and quick so one could hide behind a taller librarian or run for the business librarian when a familiar business student or faculty member approached the desk.

As the twenty-first century began, the library received more computer workstations and the World Wide Web was becoming the carrier for an increasing number of library indexes. Year-by-year, the number of CD-ROM resources went down. The data tape library vanished. Dial-up was a thing of the past, and the librarians doing mediated searching were thankful for that. The web products were easier to use and certainly more convenient for the patron. There were still some class assignments that required paper reference titles and the business questions remained challenging, but when one-stop databases such as Business OneSource arrived, the library staff breathed a collective sigh of relief. However, now there were new stressors. The workstations were much more powerful but this led to more technical questions for which library staff needed training. The class assignments that specifically required library work seemed to be down in number – we all wondered why. The reference collection stacks still had some traffic for specialized encyclopedias and the like but most of the indexes and abstracts were appearing online. There was one problem with all the online access: how to pay for the expensive databases.

Moving forward to 2006, the web was ubiquitous. The newly renovated Library West housed an IC with 135+ computers. The business librarian introduced his Virtual Business Library (now Business Library 2.0 at *http://businesslibrary.uflib.ufl.edu/*), which made a dramatic difference in how we handled business questions. Once pointed there, many business students found their own way to whatever they needed. The business librarian still had many consultations but they were more likely to be groups working on projects or individuals working on advanced research and less likely to be basic questions from undergrads. The folklore classes, the literature classes, and others no longer needed index volumes pulled from the stacks – they were instead introduced to the online databases.

As time goes by, some students with class assignments still come to the desk for help but many do not because the professor points them to the library databases or they simply search the web and hope they will find a good source. With the advent of good web authoring tools such as LibGuides, many subject specialists are developing something akin to a virtual library that creates a self-service environment. If our questions and consultations are fewer in number, we are victims of our own success. At the University of Florida over the past six months, our statistics management system shows directional statistics at the desk as 58 percent of all transactions, exceeding printing, in-depth reference, circulation, and IT questions combined. Eighty-nine percent of all in-person questions took five minutes or less, the majority taking a mere one minute or less. This is not the same reference desk anymore and we have to ask, "Should we close it?"

The debate

In the early 1990s, Jerry Campbell (1992), former Dean of Libraries at the University of Southern California, hit the news when he questioned the maintenance of the traditional reference desk model in favor of the new technologies. The debate had only begun. Many years later, Jim Rettig (2007), later to become the President of the American Library Association (ALA), organized a 2007 ACRL National Conference Session around the topic of where reference has been and where it is going. The room for this program was filled to overflowing and emotions ran high, according to attendees. The four papers presented there are frequently cited and are available in *The Reference Librarian*, 48(2), including another exhortation from Campbell for librarians to "to step back from the practice (and their love of it), to get out of their comfort zones, and take stock" (2007, p. 23). Stephen Bell (Temple) and Sarah Barbara Watstein (UCLA), engaged in a lively debate on the future of the reference desk at the Columbia University Reference Symposium in 2007. In the reformatted version of their debate, the first question the authors respond to is: "Are we *still* talking about this?" (Watstein & Bell, 2008, p. 2). We are indeed, four years later. Discussions within the profession are always valuable and when librarians are galvanized by controversy they are sometimes inspired to do something that has long been needed in their library. But in our excitement fresh from a conference, action needs to be tempered with consideration of the local situation before transplanting another institution's changes.

The new library at the UC Merced popped up in the literature from roughly 2007 to 2009 as everyone's favorite example of doing without the reference desk. However, the reality is that the entire library is a conscious reinvention of the traditional library model. This seemed both appropriate given its status as the newest research library in the University of California system and practical given budget restraints. The Library Director, Bruce Miller, wanted to return to the basics, providing information whenever and wherever the students and faculty wanted it. The physical collection is small; electronic books far outnumber print books and print journals are nonexistent except for a small browsing collection of popular magazines that the students select (Spiro & Henry, 2010). The small staff prevents a traditional approach to the workload. Services that do not need to be provided locally, such as cataloging, were outsourced by purchasing shelf-ready books. There is a computer lab on one floor, run by the campus IT Department. The website is clean and concise and geared toward mobile devices (*http://ucmercedlibrary.info*).

The decision to do without the reference desk was driven by the small staff size, but also philosophically in keeping with the mission of the library. Library staff felt it was neither efficient nor service-oriented to provide assistance only to the small percentage of the student body entering the building. Merced librarians offer on-call assistance through email, chat, and mobile phones (voice and texting), and student assistants in bright red shirts do "roving reference," providing referrals as needed to the library staff. Digital signs convey important news and information. Former UC Merced Librarian Michelle Jacobs said, "I have reached almost twice as many students as when I sat at the reference desk" (Carlson, 2007, p. 26).

It is easier to follow a non-traditional course when a library is as new as the UC Merced Library. Established libraries have a history and tradition that is hard to overcome, along with a staff that is likely to include many long-time employees and a user base that has certain expectations. Closure of an established desk will require massive advertising efforts or students and faculty will assume they simply have no support. Librarians will likely find themselves stretched even thinner with new and different outreach duties. New libraries start fresh with a staff that will help to formulate the model, or at least come in at the ground level.

In their article about a user study at the Gustavus Adolphus College in Minnesota, Gratz and Gilbert (2011) provide an excellent summary of the literature that covers reference desk service studies in the past six years or so. They discuss the several different models that seem to be in play right now and the rationale behind them. Several authors suggest that librarians are wasted behind the traditional reference desk and that their time is better spent on information literacy initiatives and academic liaison duties. There are models employing primarily student workers or paraprofessionals, some of those more hybrid with librarians staffing the desk at busier times of the day. Tiered reference services generally employ a mix of paraprofessionals and students at a strategically placed desk (usually at an entrance) that perform a triage type of service and sometimes answer basic research questions. The on-call, consultative model, similar to that of University of California Merced, is successfully in place at Dickinson College in Pennsylvania (Arndt, 2010).

Gratz and Gilbert claim that "the overwhelming majority of studies conducted favor abandoning the traditional reference desk, staffed by professional librarians, in favor of alternative methods providing assistance" (Gratz & Gilbert, 2011, p. 425). However, they also point out that instead of investigating the students' need for a reference desk, the literature often focuses on addressing the concerns of the librarians themselves. The staff of the Folke Bernadotte Memorial Library at Gustavus surveyed their students with open-ended questions designed to determine the ways they ask for help at the library. Photo diary entries and interviews were also used. The findings suggested that the reference desk was still very important to the students there (Gratz & Gilbert, 2011). In addition to learning (and following) their users' desires, the librarians at Gustavus Adolphus have collected a valuable set of demographic data that will guide their future promotion and outreach efforts.

Trying something different

The Zell B. Miller Learning Center (MLC) at the University of Georgia is another example of an organization that looked to its users and its own particular situation, finding answers by simply trying something new. The MLC is a unique learning commons facility because it resides in a separate building from the library and includes 26 general classrooms that may be reserved by teaching faculty and other groups on campus. Having visited there shortly after the 2003 opening of the building, the author recalls spaciousness and the perfect blend of the new and old. Features such as the dark cherry wood furniture and the beautiful reading room with bookshelves invite the user to experience a state-of-the-art environment that also evokes the comfortable familiarity of a traditional library. It was all created by a partnership of the University Libraries, the Enterprise Information and Technology Services (EITS), and the Center for Teaching and Learning. All three units have staff offices in the MLC. In a 2010 *Reference Services Review* article, Barratt, Acheson, & Luken (2010) reported that gate counts surpassed 2 million, averaging 6000 visitors per day. If gate counts were all that mattered, the library staff could assume that the MLC is a rousing success. However, the librarians at the MLC were dissatisfied by the level of activity at the service desks despite constant advertising. They tried a variety of signs and postings, including the unusual method of a newsletter posted in the bathroom stalls. In addition, they used Facebook, Twitter, and campus broadcast methods (Barratt et al., 2010).

In an attempt to increase reference traffic, a new reference desk was installed in 2006 in a very central location. This brought the count to five public service desks, four of them staffed by student technology consultants. Despite the new and highly visible desk, in-person reference statistics remained low. Since implementing a browser-based instant messaging service, chat reference activity had climbed and the two largest libraries (Main and Science) maintained their high level of in-person reference activity as well. The MLC desks were busy with technical and directional questions but ready reference and in-depth reference were very low, reaching levels of only about 2.2 percent of all questions in 2008, compared to 42–47 percent in the Main and Science libraries (Barratt et al., 2010, p. 47).

The librarian instruction team at the MLC decided in spring 2009 to experiment with some different service models. They tried roving reference for a period of two weeks, creation of a service outpost for another two weeks at the MLC's Jittery Joe's coffee shop, and outreach for four nights a week at four dormitories. According to Barratt et al. (2010), the experiments had mixed results, all of which are reported in detail in the article. The statistics were not high, but the librarians learned a lot about the research habits of the students and their awareness (or lack thereof) of library services.

Each April, the MLC staff conducts a survey to evaluate how patrons are using the library services and resources. In 2009, after the outpost experiences, the survey was comprised of only three questions that explored whether the students had research projects assigned and, if so, their preferences for finding sources and help when needed. Eighty percent of the respondents had research projects and they were about equally divided between asking their peers, asking their professors or teaching assistants, consulting a librarian, or not asking at all. Of those who asked a librarian, their first choice was to ask in-person (Barratt et al., 2010).

Overall, it was decided that the outreach had served as an excellent way to raise the profile of librarians on campus in general and, specifically, awareness of the research assistance service at the MLC. Barrett et al. (2010) reported that they would continue to experiment with different reference models but on the basis of the survey, no major changes were made to the in-person service. Other plans included investigation of research consultation scheduling, exploration of a possible consultation desk located next to the Research Assistance desk, and making a bigger effort to get out from behind the desk to keep in touch with the patrons and how they are using the Center. The MLC instruction team members are not unique solely because they tried new models, but what is noteworthy is that they conducted their experiment in a relatively short timeframe and they tried several methods at once. They did not hesitate to report their results, evaluate the successes and failures, and plan future endeavors accordingly. In short, they demonstrated the flexibility for which their facility is noted.

Finally, it might not be such a bad idea to keep that reference desk in nearby storage. An interesting development has recently occurred at the University of Southern California's Doheny Library where a hybrid model of the reference desk is returning almost 20 years after Jerry Campbell so vehemently spoke for its obsolescence and put the University of Southern California Libraries on a different path. This was done not on a whim, but rather after thoughtful traffic analysis and consideration of user feedback. At the ACRL 2011 virtual conference, Tompson and Quinlan said that the demand for personalized service at the Doheny Library has exceeded their expectations and "as a renaissance was experienced in the Libraries reference operations with the re-introduction of the reference desk in the *L.A. Times* Reference Room, so has a revitalization emerged across the Libraries' service" (Tompson and Quinlan, 2011). Fear of failure or unexpected outcomes has no place in a nimble organization. Successful approaches to reference service take into account student opinions and faculty advice, analysis of usage statistics, consideration of the availability of library staff resources, and staff satisfaction that the time at the desk is well spent. When the unknown becomes the known to us, we cross the divide.

It's about the librarian too

In the end, the issue is not about the furniture. The point is to determine a course of action that fits the needs of the specific library's clientele and at the same time to realistically acknowledge the library's ability to sustain whatever model is chosen with a high level of service quality. This is a balancing act. As a long-time practicing public service librarian, this author must admit that removal of the traditional reference desk resonates, particularly after reading the words of Scott Kennedy at the Homer Babbidge Library, University of Connecticut. Kennedy calls the reference desk "a physical and metaphorical barrier" that "does anything but welcome and invite participatory learning" (Kennedy, 2011, p. 324). The Homer Babbidge Library staff plans to replace the desk with smaller tables. The strategic placement of assistance points throughout the library suits the learning paradigm currently in place within most higher education institutions where knowledge is not so much absorbed from a source of authority but created within a group of peers who could most certainly benefit from the advice of a librarian consultant located nearby. The monolithic desk literally separates the librarian from the student and reinforces the authority-to-supplicant nature of the transaction. It seems at odds with the environment of collaboration and point-of-need assistance. The smaller or portable unit provides a comfortable space that invites the client to sit down and make the connection with someone who can help.

The loneliness of the reference librarian behind the desk creates a morale problem that needs to be addressed. Marie Radford speaks and writes passionately of the need to convince ourselves as a profession that we add value to the research process. The University of Southern California Doheny Library experience demonstrates the revitalization of service that can occur when the staff feels a change is for the better. Radford suggests that we can alleviate our own anxiety and at the same time make a greater impact on our customers by making a personal commitment to excellence in reference services. She reminds us that "Library users know (and respond in kind) when service is given enthusiastically (or grudgingly)" (Radford, 2008, p. 112). Librarians can do much to reconnect by simply listening and responding. However, there is much to distract and worry us. Radford warns us that the dedicated librarian, whether young or old, who tries to keep on top of all the changes and new technologies and at the same time spends long hours providing service, sometimes in several different formats, is in great risk of burnout. She suggests that the team approach (calling when you need help) and a break or short sabbatical for public service staff can do wonders to maintain good service.

Ross T. LaBaugh (2008) suggests a look at the counselor librarian concept first reported by David K. Maxfield of the University of Illinois, Chicago in the 1950s. The University of Illinois, Chicago's Counselor Librarianship program was a re-envisioned approach to traditional reference, incorporating general education, library instruction, reference services and student counseling. If this program sounds familiar, it is because the modern IC exemplifies a similar philosophy in today's library, striving to help and connect with students in more than just traditional research assistance. It may well be the right time to revisit some of Maxfield's ideas and return to a more personal, therapeutic model that focuses on listening to the patron and responding to their question, not just as the reference librarian who can help them find the best key words to enter in the search box, but rather as someone who understands the challenges of the academic environment and can help the client connect with the right resources. In this model, it's about the reference librarian, not the reference desk.

Conclusion

The representative models in this chapter demonstrate the importance of the partnerships and the patrons, nurtured and sustained under the umbrella of a clearly stated mission that arises from the expressed needs of the students, the teaching faculty, and the librarians. It's worth noting that by comparison to student assessments, the needs and the advice of the teaching faculty appears to be under-represented in the literature. The expanded commons, by whatever name it is called, is just getting underway in many libraries and time will tell what kind of collaborations will come to the forefront and what the learning outcome measures will tell us about the success of those partnerships. Closer relationships with other campus departments and offices have the added benefit of increasing the library's visibility and participation in the overall learning and teaching mission of the university, as well as fostering greater understanding between the different cultures on campus.

We have successfully drawn the student body to the IC. In the next chapter, Steven Carrico and Ann Lindell of the University of Florida Libraries will take a closer look at the physical design of some newly created or remodeled IC. They will explore the "Wow!" factor and how it relates to the overall experience of the users. But librarians also need to figure out how to keep the students in the library and, better yet, to convince them that we are part of the learning process. Perhaps the knowledge that assistance is available would come from something as simple as a greeting, a little more visibility on the floor, and a pleasant first encounter at the front desk.

Think about what brings you back repeatedly to the same retail establishment: quality products that you need and probably some you didn't know you need that entice you once you get there; an easy shopping experience; good service; good value. We need to work on the ease of shopping with better signs and more visual cues, a better catalog, true discovery systems, and in-house communication systems. It is perplexing that IC librarians have not more diligently pursued in-house call systems that would facilitate getting help to the customers when and where they need it. How many IC have the help desk phone number prominently posted at every workstation, or have considered a call button? Every student has a cellphone so why don't we focus on getting an "Ask for Help" number in their directory? Why isn't the chat reference button embedded in our web pages and databases? Yes, the library resources are increasingly self-service, but just like the clerk assigned to the self-checkout aisle in the grocery store, we can hover nearby, virtually or in-person, to ease the way.

References

Arndt, T. S. (2010). Reference service without the desk. *Reference Services Review*, *38*(1), 71–80. DOI: 10.1108/00907321011020734

Barratt, C. C., Acheson, P., & Luken, E. (2010). Reference models in the electronic library: The Miller Center at the University of Georgia. *Reference Services Review*, *38*(1), 44–56. DOI: 10.1108/00907321011020716

Beagle, D. R. (2006). *The information commons handbook*. New York: Neal-Schuman Publishers.

Beagle, D. R. (2012, 12 January). Genesis of the models [listserv communication]. Retrieved from *http://listserv.binghamton.edu/scripts/wa.exe?A1=ind1201&L=INFOCOMMONS-L*

Beatty, S. (2010). Information commons, University of Calgary: Providing service through collaboration and integration. *Journal of Library Administration*, *50*(2), 145–159. DOI: 10.1080/01930820903455008

Campbell, J. (1992). Shaking the conceptual foundations of reference: A perspective. *RSR: Reference Services Review*, *20*(4), 29–36.

Campbell, J. (2007). Still shaking the shaking the conceptual foundations of reference: A perspective. *The Reference Librarian*, *48*(2), 21–24. DOI: 10.1300/J120v48n02_05

Carlson, S. (2007). Are reference desks dying out? Librarians struggle to redefine – and in some cases eliminate – the venerable institution. *The Reference Librarian*, *48*(2), 25–30. DOI: 10.1300/J120v48n02_06

Dewey, B. I. (2008). Circle of service: A collaborative information commons planning model. In B. Schader (Ed.), *Learning commons: Evolution and collaborative essentials* (pp. 37–67). Oxford: Chandos Publishing.

Dewey, B. I., & Little, J. K. (2006). *Circle of service: The commons at the University of Tennessee* [PowerPoint slides]. Retrieved from *http://works.bepress.com/barbara_dewey/8*

EDUCAUSE Learning Initiative (ELI). (2011). *7 Things you should know about the Modern Learning Commons*. Retrieved from *http://www.educause.edu/ELI7Things*

Getis, V., Gynn, C., & Metros, S. (2006). The Digital Union: The Ohio State University. In D. B. Oblinger (Ed.), *Learning spaces* (Chapter 31). EDUCAUSE. Retrieved from *http://www.educause.edu/LearningSpaces*

Gratz, A., & Gilbert, J. (2011). Meeting student needs at the reference desk. *Reference Services Review*, *39*(3), 423–438. DOI: 10.1108/00907321111161412

Kennedy, S. (2011). Farewell to the reference librarian. *Journal of Library Administration*, *51*(4), 319–325. DOI: 10.1080/01930826.2011.556954

LaBaugh, R. T. (2008). Solution focused reference: Counselor librarianship revisited. In M. L. Madden & S. K. Steiner (Eds.), *The desk and beyond: Next generation reference services* (pp. 38–52). Chicago: Association of College and Research Libraries.

Lippincott, J. K. (2006). Linking the information commons to learning. In D. B. Oblinger (Ed.), *Learning spaces* (Chapter 7). USA: EDUCAUSE. Retrieved from *http://www.educause.edu/LearningSpaces*

Lotts, M., & Graves, S. (2011). Using the iPad for reference services: Librarians go mobile. *College & Research Libraries News*, *72*(4), 217–220. Retrieved from *http://crl.acrl.org/*

MacDonald, J., & McCabe, K. (2011, 11 April). iRoam: Leveraging mobile technology to provide innovative point of need reference service. *Code4Lib Journal*, *13*. Retrieved from *http://journal.code4lib.org/issues/issue13*

Martell, C. (2007). The elusive user: Changing use patterns in academic libraries. *College & Research Libraries*, *68*(5), 435–444. Retrieved from *http://crl.acrl.org/*

Mendelsohn, H. (2012). University of Central Florida's Campus Connections Program. *Reference Services Review*, *40*(1), 116–124. DOI: 10.1108/009073 21211203676

Molholt, P. (1985). On converging paths: The computing center and the library. *Journal of Academic Librarianship*, *11*, 284–288. Retrieved from *https://search.ebscohost.com/login.aspx?direct=true&db=llf&AN=50272270 9&site=ehost-live*

Murphy, S. (2010, 24 September). Vocera project ending January 1, 2011 [blog post]. Retrieved from *http://library.osu.edu/blogs/communication/2010/09/24/vocera-project-ending-january-1-2011/*

Novotny, E. (Comp.). (2002). *Reference Service Statistics & Assessment*. ARL SPEC kit 268. Washington, DC: Association of Research Libraries, Office of Leadership and Management Services.

Plane, R. A. (1982). Merging a library and a computing center. *Perspectives in Computing*, 2(3), 14–21.

Radford, M. L. (2008). A personal choice: Reference service excellence. *Reference & User Services Quarterly*, 48(2), 108, 110–115. Retrieved from *http://rusa.metapress.com/content/L74261/*

Radford, M. L. (2011, March). *A future in transition: Foreseeing forthcoming opportunities & challenges in academic reference*. Preview webcast for the Association of College and Research Libraries (ACRL) 2011 Virtual Conference, Philadelphia, PA. Retrieved from *http://www.acrl.ala.org/acrlinsider/archives/3192*

Rettig, J. (2007). The reference question – where has reference been? Where is reference going? *The Reference Librarian*, 48(2). DOI: 10.1300/J120v48n02_04

Scharf, M., & Chabot, L. (2011, April). *Listening to users … Closing the feedback loop: Just do it!* Paper presented at the Association of College and Research Libraries (ACRL) 2011 Virtual Conference, Philadelphia, PA. Retrieved from *http://www.learningtimes.net/acrl/2011/day2-session4/*

Spiro, L., & Henry, G. (2010). Can a new research library be all-digital? In Council on Library and Information Resources (Ed.), *The Idea of Order: Transforming Research Collections for 21st Century Scholarship* (pp. 5–80). CLIR publication no. 147. Washington, DC: CLIR.

Tompson, S., & Quinlan, C. (2011, April). *Reference desk renaissance: Connecting with users in the digital age*. Paper presented at the Association of College and Research Libraries (ACRL) 2011 Virtual Conference, Philadelphia, PA. Retrieved from *http://www.ala.org/acrl/sites/ala.org.acrl/files/content/conferences/confsandpreconfs/national/2011/papers/reference_desk.pdf*

University of Washington Libraries. (n.d.). What is the Research Commons? Retrieved from *http://commons.lib.washington.edu/about*

Watstein, S. B., & Bell, S. J. (2008). Is there a future for the reference desk? A point–counterpoint discussion. *The Reference Librarian*, 49(1), 1–20. DOI: 10.1080/02763870802103258

Additional resources

Accardi, M. T., Cordova, M., & Leeder, K. (2010). Reviewing the library learning commons: History, models, and perspectives. *College & Undergraduate Libraries*, 17(2/3), 310–329. Retrieved from *http://www.tandfonline.com/loi/wcul20*

Bailey, D. R. (2009). Bibliography: The information commons and beyond. *Library Commons Basics*, Paper 4. Retrieved from *http://digitalcommons. providence.edu/lib_commons_basics/4/*

Bailey, D. R., & Tierney, B. G. (2008). *Transforming library service through information commons: Case studies for the digital age.* Chicago: American Library Association.

Beatty, S., & White, P. (2005). Information commons: Models for e-lit and the integration of learning. *JeLit: Journal of eLiteracy*, 2(1). Retrieved from *http://www.jelit.org/tocJun2005.html*

Forrest, C., & Halbert, C. (Eds.). (2009). *A field guide to the information commons.* Lanham, MD: Scarecrow Press.

Haas, L., & Robertson, J. (2004). *The information commons.* ARL SPEC kit 281. Washington, DC: Association of Research Libraries, Office of Leadership and Management Services.

Held, T. (2009). The information and learning commons: A selective guide to sources. *Reference Services Review*, 37(2), 190–206. DOI: 10.1108/0090732 0910957224

Kranich, N. (2002). *The information commons: Selected bibliography.* Retrieved from *http://www.ala.org/offices/oitp/publications/infocommons0204/ kranichbib*

Lippincott, J. K. (2010). Information commons: Meeting millennials' needs. *Journal of Library Administration*, 50(1), 27–37. DOI: 10.1080/019308209 03422156

Schader, B. (Ed.). (2008). *Learning commons: Evolution and collaborative essentials.* Oxford: Chandos.

Vyhanek, K., & Zlatos, C. (2011). *Reconfiguring service delivery.* ARL SPEC kit 327. Washington, DC: Association of Research Libraries.

3

A post-occupancy look at library building renovations: meeting the needs of the twenty-first century users

Steven Carrico and Ann Lindell

Abstract: This chapter explores recently renovated or newly constructed library buildings, with an emphasis on features contributing to the user experience. The authors summarize the current library literature focused on library buildings and renovations and responses to these new facilities from library workers and users. Results of three related surveys, conducted during fall semester, 2011, are presented and analyzed. Six building profiles, based on site visits to recently constructed or renovated libraries in Florida and Georgia are shared as examples of current trends. In conclusion, the authors offer observations about the future of library buildings and recommendations to consider in the building design process.

Key words: academic libraries, architectural design – evaluation, facility design and construction, information commons (IC), libraries – space utilization, libraries and students, library architecture, library buildings – remodelling, library buildings – design and construction, library planning.

> "Design buildings according to how people actually behave, not according to how you think they should behave."

– J. Schallen, (Comp.). (n.d.) Practical tips for building design

Introduction

Academic libraries in the early twenty-first century face a challenge to remain relevant in an online, interactive age. The academic library building historically was a center for academic research and communication. In the 1870s Charles William Eliot, President of Harvard University, reportedly observed the library was "the heart of the university" (Dunlap, 1995). While libraries still function as repositories for knowledge and offer a plethora of services to provide access and delivery of information, they now offer an ever increasing number of online resources and services so patrons often need not physically enter a library building. This dilemma presents a challenge to the essential identity and function of academic libraries. With a lack of infrastructure for new technology and physical layouts that reflect an older library model of book-lined shelves and solitary study, libraries can be perceived by many students, faculty, and administrators as antiquated and superfluous. There is no question that the online environment has drastically changed how patrons access resources and perform research. Because libraries continue to value service as a core mission, to remain relevant they must adopt new modes of delivery and reinvent their physical spaces.

Across the profession, arguments continue about what role the academic library building should play on campus. Libraries continue to serve as spaces for knowledgeable staff to provide the traditional functions of classification, preservation and storage and delivery of essential books, journals, and a variety of other media that support university research and coursework. However, opinions differ widely on whether brick-and-mortar library buildings still serve an essential function on campus. There are divergent views even among library administrators. For example, Suzanne Thorin, the Dean of Libraries at Syracuse University, said this about the library as place: "let's face it: the library, as a place, is dead" (Kolowich, 2009). Richard Luce, Director of University Libraries at Emory University, countered this sentiment by stating that users come to libraries "to interact with one another – to talk, to collaborate, to think, to communicate, to be with one another" (Kolowich, 2009). It is clear that for the academic library to continue to claim its stake as the center or heart of the university, it must prove itself as an essential space for discovery, collaboration, and sharing of ideas. The library must be perceived as an integral element of the academic experience and an essential space to its users.

To retool its traditional role, many universities have recently undergone renovations of existing library space, erected new library buildings, or are developing new building projects, all hoping to bring in students and users, placate university faculty and administrators, and attract donors. Shill & Tonner (2004) reported 390 building projects launched between January 1995 and December 2002. In 2009 the Association of Research Libraries (ARL) issued a report detailing how 66 academic libraries in the USA and Canada erected new buildings or remodeled library space in 2008 (ARL, 2009). The growing importance of this topic has moved the American Library Association (ALA) to devote an entire webpage to library buildings, construction, and launching library renovations, with dozens of resources listed and continuously updated (ALA, 2011).

Why the flurry of building construction in libraries? According to Shill & Tonner (2004), survey results reveal new library facilities are working, drawing in users as never before: "In general, students are using new and improved libraries at levels greater than their use of preproject library facilities" (p. 127). Yet, most of the literature and resources made available on erecting new library buildings or conducting renovations focus more on the pre-project preparation and seldom on the post-occupancy "lessons learned." To that end, this chapter focuses on this crucial phase of library building projects: looking back to determine what worked and what did not work in newly built or remodeled library buildings. The authors consulted recent literature in several cognate disciplines (library science, education, design) to gain an awareness of recent library construction projects, and to identify studies that emphasized post-occupancy assessments or methodologies for conducting such assessments. As illustration, the authors provide six 'profiles' based on visits to recently renovated or newly constructed academic library spaces in Florida and Georgia. Additionally, the chapter analyzes the results of three related surveys that were administered to librarians, library staff, and library users. These surveys, in whole or in part, solicited feedback and opinions from staff and users about the success and failures of their new library facility. It is hoped that the information presented here will provide some insight to librarians and administrators who are planning building projects in the near future.

Literature review

There is a wealth of literature devoted to design and construction of new library buildings and developing renovations of existing facilities. The past few years have seen library organizations issue reports or articles focusing on libraries of the next generation, including the "Top Ten

Assumptions for the Future of Academic Libraries and Librarians," as determined and ranked by the Association of College and Research Libraries' (ACRL) Research Committee in 2007 (Mullins, Allen, & Hufford, 2007). In 2010, ACRL's Research Planning & Review Committee issued its own "2010 Top Ten Trends in Academic Libraries" (ACRL, 2010). The Association of Southeastern Research Libraries' Education Committee issued a report titled *Shaping the Future: ASERL's Competencies for Research Libraries* (ASERL, 2000). Not to be outdone, the Council on Library & Information Resources (CLIR) issued a paper from meetings of library experts, *No Brief Candle: Reconceiving Research Libraries for the 21st Century* (CLIR, 2008).

Journal articles devoted to the future library and library buildings include those published by Allen (2011), Bennett (2006), Collins (1999), Conley (2006), Grose (2010), Kolowich (2011), and Lewis (2007), which are all excellent think pieces on how physical buildings are being adapted or completely reinvented for the next generation of library users. *The Learning Commons: Seven Simple Steps to Transform Your Library*, (Harland, 2011) is a valid source for conducting a renovation for a Learning Commons. Additionally, three articles (Fox & Stuart, 2009; Spencer, 2007; and Lynn, 2011) detail specific library building projects centered on newly designed information commons (IC), and provide insights on the factors involved in creating an effective learning environment.

Noteworthy monographs published on the design and construction of innovative library buildings include *Interior Design for Libraries* (Brown, 2002), *The Library as Place* (Buschman and Leckie, 2007), *Libraries Designed for Users* (Lushington, 2002), *The Academic Library Building in the Digital Age: A Study of Construction, Planning, and Design of New Library Space* (Stewart, 2010), and *Libraries as Places: Buildings for the 21st Century* (Bisbrouck, Desjardins, Menil, Ponce, & Rouyer-Gayett, 2004). Although somewhat dated, *Academic Libraries as High-Tech Gateways* (Bazillion & Braun, 1995) is still a useful guide for libraries in the early planning stages of any building project. Likewise, *Countdown to a New Library* (Woodward, 2010), *The Library Renovation, Maintenance, and Construction Handbook* (Barclay & Scott, 2011), *Checklist of Library Building Design Considerations* (Sannwald, 2001), and *Managing Your Library Construction Project* (McCarthy, 2007) are all very valuable as "checklists" of issues and features to consider when launching a new building or renovation project.

The design literature provides an excellent, often highly pictorial, showcase of recently constructed library building projects, but also includes writings on post-occupancy studies in general. While some design monographs outline general evaluative methodologies for practitioners of both design and construction, there is little specifically targeted to library facilities. An exception is the article "Quantitative (GIS) and qualitative (BPE) assessments of library performance" (Preiser & Wang, 2008), which concentrates its discourse on public libraries, but also addresses methodologies for evidence-based, master planning of facilities and the assessment of library spaces that can be generalized to the academic environment.

While resources focusing on post-occupancy of library buildings are not particularly plentiful, a few are extremely helpful for librarians. Lackney and Zajfen (2005) conducted a post-occupancy assessment of their library in Saudi Arabia, while Hassanain and Mudhei (2006) used renovations in three public libraries as case studies to determine how the buildings met their intended pre-construction goals of meeting user needs and services. Adhami (2011) conducted an extensive post-occupancy study on the massive renovation of the University of Florida's Library West and offers excellent overviews of the process and steps to consider, including the incorporation of user and staff survey results into the findings. And finally, Kusack's (1991) *Evaluating Library Buildings: Principles and Procedures for Post-occupancy Evaluation* details the methodologies, evaluation design considerations, and data collection tactics he recommends for libraries when conducting post-occupancy evaluations (Kusack, 1991).

Six library building profiles

The following six building profiles focus on a variety of recent renovation and building projects in Florida and Georgia. The first three profiles are examples of libraries that redesigned and remodeled space within existing library buildings. The fourth and fifth profiles provide examples of larger-scale renovations encompassing entire existing library buildings. The sixth profile is devoted to a newly erected state-of-the-art building designed as a shared, campus-wide "Learning Commons" managed by a university library. All six libraries were visited by one or both authors. Each visit included an interview with librarians and staff regarding the building projects pre-construction and post-occupancy.

University of Central Florida Libraries

Figure 3.1   University of Central Florida: Knowledge Commons

Building project: Renovation
Completed: 2010
Original building erected: 1968, renovated 1984
Space renovated: Main Library/Knowledge Commons
Features of the new space: Seating for 479 students; lounge areas and furniture; individual and collaborative workstations; increased natural lighting; consultation spaces
Summary: The renovated space at University of Central Florida Libraries created a "Knowledge Commons" on the second floor of the main library building. Included is a redesigned research information desk with adjacent consultation cubicles for in-depth librarian/patron research consultations. Computing areas feature modular, movable furnishings to accommodate both the solitary

researcher and groups working together on projects (see Figure 3.1). Additional spaces feature more comfortable chairs and sofas. Most study/work areas are infused during daylight hours with natural light from surrounding windows. Whiteboards (both static and portable) are plentiful. Incorporated into the overall design is a cafe, with an adjacent seating area and popular reading collection. Attractive signage with a consistent visual design provides way-finding assistance throughout the space.

Georgia Tech University (1)

Figure 3.2 Georgia Tech University: West Commons

Figure 3.3 Georgia Tech University: detail of suspended power cable

Building project: Renovation – West and East Commons
Completed: West – 2002, 2 West – 2009; East – 2005
Original building erected: West – 1960s; East – 1970s
Space renovated: Circulation/Reference/Study Space, two stories; East – 8000 sq. ft
Features of the new space: Combined Reference/Circulation/ Reserves; collaborative spaces; hi-tech computer workstations; flexible areas with mobile furniture and sliding, pull-down plug-ins for laptops; multimedia and presentation studios; gallery and exhibit space
Summary: Through three phases of renovation, the Georgia Tech Library created two innovative and attractive commons areas inside two older library buildings. The first phase created the West Commons on the first floor inside the main library (see Figure 3.2). The second phase created the East Commons on the first floor of Crosland Tower. The third phase renovated the second floor of the main library creating a collaborative space, "2 West," as an extension of the West Commons. One notable aspect of both the

East Commons project and the West Commons renovation was how the library employed multiple online surveys and focus groups to solicit input from students and other library users. The resulting designs, which incorporated a significant amount of feedback received from users, includes increased collaborative work space, better artificial and natural lighting throughout the study spaces, and easily movable, modular furniture. An excellent example of this flexible design can be found in the East Commons, as it offers movable extension outlets suspended from the ceiling, a feature that allows users to sit with a laptop anywhere in the room while having easy access to a power outlet (see Figure 3.3). 2 West provides several collaborative study areas partitioned by screens and large tables for meetings and group activities.

Florida State College at Jacksonville (FL) – North Campus

Figure 3.4 Florida State College at Jacksonville: Circle of Learning

Figure 3.5 Florida State College at Jacksonville: Study Room

Building project: Renovation

Completed: 2010

Original building erected: 1970

Space renovated: Main Library (shared space). Overall – 17 000 sq. ft; library portion – 9000 sq. ft

Features of the new space: Learning Commons; shared space (library, student success center, tutoring center); classrooms for non-library instruction; a combined Reference/Circulation Desk; enclosed collaborative spaces with glass and white board walls; reduced library stacks

Summary: Following a statewide initiative to provide "student success centers" on state college campuses to aid "students at risk," the Florida State College at Jacksonville North Campus Library was completely renovated and enlarged to include library space (with a smaller footprint than pre-renovation), the Student Success Center, and the Tutoring Center. The "Circle of Learning" in the center of the space functions both as intermittent classroom and open computer lab (see Figure 3.4). Additional features include academic classrooms, a faculty resource center, and glass-enclosed group study rooms with interior walls that function as white boards (see Figure 3.5). An existing rectangular space was redesigned to include all of these components in a perceived circular arrangement, with separate entrances at four "corners." The library utilizes a consolidated circulation/reference desk from which staff monitor two of the four entrances. As the stacks space was reduced, the library staff significantly weeded its onsite print collections and collection development is now focused on obtaining digital materials when possible.

University of North Florida

Figure 3.6 University of North Florida: Reading Room

Building project: Renovation

Completed: 2005

Original building erected: 1980

Space renovated: Thomas G. Carpenter Library (Main Library), 199 000 sq. ft

Features of the new space: Circulation and Reference areas on two separate floors; group study rooms; large glass walls and improved lighting; stacks redesign; appealing outdoor landscape; extensive art collection (donated by regional artists and collectors) displayed throughout the building

Summary: The Thomas G. Carpenter Library at the University of North Florida was renovated in phases while the building remained open and in service. The first floor (incorporating the main entrance) includes a service point for circulation and reserves. This area accommodates high foot traffic and serves as a place for undergraduates to meet and collaborate. The Reference Desk, previously located on the first floor, was relocated to the second floor as the noise levels and congestion on the first floor were extremely distracting during reference consultations. The renovated library is open-plan and study spaces are illuminated by plentiful natural light that streams from a series of large windows located throughout the building (see Figure 3.6). The second-floor IC area contains over 325 computer workstations for patron use. Two large library classrooms, each equipped with 40 computer workstations for hands-on instruction can be joined by retracting a modular wall to create one large classroom space. These classrooms, when not in use for instruction, can be opened to allow for additional general computing access during times of peak demand. In addition to the reference desk, a custom service desk was built and located near the computing area with the intention of providing assistance with printing and computing, and staffed by student employees. Subsequent changes in funding altered this plan. The library administration is currently cultivating partnerships with campus IT to address patron computing service needs within the building.

University of Florida

Figure 3.7   University of Florida: Library West Entrance

Figure 3.8   University of Florida: Library West Ground Floor

Building project: Renovation

Completed: 2006

Original building erected: 1967

Space renovated: Library West (Main Library), 89 000 sq. ft

Features of the new space: Information commons (IC); compact shelving; escalator entrance; increased seating and workstations; café; study carrels; compact shelving in most stacks areas; enclosed group study and high-tech media rooms; graduate-only floor

Summary: Library West was closed for over two years while the existing structure was gutted and completely renovated, and a 30 000 sq. ft addition was erected. A noticeable feature of the new building is its entrance design on the ground floor, which includes a revolving glass door and two large escalators – one for incoming users, and one for exiting users (see Figure 3.7). Also located on the ground floor near the entrance are a coffee shop and a lounge-style area with various seating options. Users must enter the building on the ground floor and ride an escalator or elevator to the second floor, where they have access to collections and services on six floors via elevators and stairwells. Staff members report that the escalators have frequent downtime, necessitating detours through the ground floor stacks area to reach other parts of the building. Interior finishes such as cork flooring, hanging light fixtures, and hard-surfaced walls were chosen both for aesthetic purposes and to achieve sustainability standards. Flooring in the main service areas had to be replaced fairly quickly because of durability issues. Service areas and most open study spaces are located to take advantage of plentiful natural light sources. The library maintains two main service points: a circulation/reserves/information desk on the second floor, and a research assistance desk on the third floor near the large IC. The IC includes large banks of computer workstations, group study rooms, high-tech media studios, and an adaptable performance/event space. While some research materials are located in these areas, the bulk of the library collection is housed in compact shelving on the ground floor (see Figure 3.8). A popular feature of the building is its "graduate-student-only" sixth floor study area, which is accessible to this population by ID card swipe. Increased noise levels (post-renovation) have been an issue because of the hard interior surfaces and vertical open areas near the two-story curtain wall, which allows sound to filter up from the front entrance, the coffee shop, and the escalators. Way-finding is often a challenge as well because most collections are on the ground floor, while service points and exit paths are on upper levels.

Georgia Tech University (2)

Figure 3.9 Georgia Tech University: Clough Undergraduate Learning Commons, exterior

Figure 3.10 Georgia Tech University: Clough Undergraduate Learning Commons, green roof structure

Building project: New building

Completed: 2011

Space created: Clough Undergraduate Learning Commons, 220000 sq. ft

Features of the new building: 2000 seats; shared space – instructional centers housed inside the building; hi-tech labs, classrooms, and collaborative spaces; walls of glass; industrial design

Summary: This very large new building includes the Learning Commons but also houses centers for instructional tutoring and advising, and includes the Office of Undergraduate Studies. Designed for undergraduate users, this ultra-modern, innovative building (US Green Building Council (USGBC) Leadership in Energy and Environmental Design (LEED) Platinum rating pending) embraces numerous environmentally sustainable features such as a 1.4 million gallon water cistern, solar energy panels, and green roof structure (see Figures 3.9 and 3.10). The Learning Commons facility is managed by the library and the campus's main library is adjacent and connected to the commons by a shared corridor. The Learning Commons has one service desk on the first floor that provides general information to the building; and although managed by the main library, the facility does not offer a reference service. Instead, users needing library or research assistance must travel to the adjacent building to consult with librarians. Conversely, the university's central IT department does offer a variety of onsite services for users, fielding many questions and offering a problem-solving service most hours of the day.

Observations about the six profiles

Whether examining a new building, as in the case of the Clough Commons at Georgia Tech Library (the last building profile), or a renovation of existing space (the first five building profiles), we found each of the profiled libraries offered attractive, vibrant spaces. One measure of success is building use: all five of the renovated libraries saw a surge in the number of users as captured by pre- and post-occupancy gate counts. All of the profiled buildings make generous use of natural day lighting and/or provide stylish lighting fixtures. In particular, the University of North Florida Library and the Georgia Tech West Commons provide excellent examples of using large windows to create a sense of openness and provide an abundance of natural light. All of the profiled new buildings offered a variety of functional space with innovated features for the twenty-first century library user. During the renovations to create additional user space, two of the libraries – the University of Florida and the Florida State College – relocated book stacks to less public areas in the building or to off-campus storage facilities.

While many features in the five renovations are aimed at attracting undergraduate students (modular furnishings, updated equipment, collaborative spaces), nowhere is this more apparent than at Georgia Tech's East Commons, with its mobile, lightweight furniture and movable overhead electrical outlets. While all six libraries offer extensive computing facilities, some layouts are more successful than others.

Georgia Tech and the University of Florida have IC areas that seem spacious compared to those at the other three profiled schools. Part of this is accomplished by the choice of furnishings, but in some cases it is the patron demand for access to computing equipment that necessitates locating more than the optimal amount of equipment into space available. The libraries at the University of North Florida and the University of Central Florida both provide several spaces with lounge-style furniture to create comfortable reading spaces and accommodate more informal groups. Offering collaborative study rooms and areas is also a prominent feature of all six buildings, as the popularity of these spaces is noted by staff. Aside from the hive-like quality of the IC areas in all of the libraries, there is also evidence of the need for quiet spaces, given the popularity of the glass-enclosed reading rooms at the University of North Florida and the graduate-student-only floor at the University of Florida's Library West.

Survey results

Three surveys were developed to solicit feedback to questions regarding user and staff satisfaction or dissatisfaction on library space and a variety of features found in library buildings. The first survey tool ("New Library Spaces – Post-Occupancy Survey," see the appendix to this chapter) was drafted to acquire feedback from staff working in US and Canadian academic libraries that had undergone new building or renovated library projects. This survey asked staff to respond to questions about the physical space and design elements in their library facilities. Additionally, a set of two related surveys were developed by the team of Crump/Freund – "Library Staff Survey" and "Library User Survey" (see Appendices A and B at the end of this volume) – which gathered responses from both staff and users in five US academic libraries. The Crump/Freund surveys focused on user services being offered to library patrons but did garner insightful feedback from users and staff regarding the libraries as place.

The "New Library Spaces – Post-Occupancy Survey" yielded 36 responses from staff working in 17 different academic institutions. The majority of respondents (33) reported they were employed by their institutions both before and after construction took place, which provides a pre-construction and post-occupancy comparison. Seventy-five percent of respondents replied that staff had input on planning and design in the pre-construction phase of the new building or renovation, and 80 percent replied that staff had input during the post-occupancy implementation phase. However, most telling were the narrative comments that respondents provided. Out of the 22 narrative comments collected in the survey, 16 respondents indicated that input was solicited from staff in the design phase but reported that very little of their feedback was actually incorporated into the final plans. Five respondents did state that staff had input into the design and physical features included in their new buildings (one respondent was unsure). Of the 17 narrative comments collected in the survey asking staff if they had input on features after the building project was complete, seven indicated their feedback went largely ignored, five were unsure, and five responded that some changes were made based on staff feedback. However, the majority of respondents stated that any post-occupancy changes made to facilities were relatively minor (e.g. changing of computer locations, repositioning lighting), while concerns relating to the lack of functionality and maintenance of major fixtures and the physical layout of service spaces go largely unaddressed.

When staff were asked to rate physical features (amount of user space, lighting, noise levels, and so on) most of the feedback reveals that the majority of the respondents (54 percent) indicated they were satisfied with their new facility, while only 26 percent were dissatisfied, and 20 percent were neutral. One element (noise levels in study and office space) did receive a split result: 44 percent indicated they were satisfied while 42 percent were dissatisfied, and 14 percent were neutral. Most respondents were positive about the functional and aesthetic (materials used in the building, attractiveness of design, and so on) features of the new buildings: 57 percent were satisfied while only 28 percent were dissatisfied, and 15 percent were neutral. The exception to this are responses on the topic of temperature and ventilation, with 47 percent indicating they were dissatisfied with these elements vs. 36 percent who were satisfied, and 17 percent who were neutral.

Overall, while the majority of staff who responded to the "New Library Spaces – Post-Occupancy Survey" felt their input was not solicited or not incorporated in both the design and post-occupancy phases of the building projects, the survey does show that most staff respondents were quite positive in rating the physical features, functionality, and aesthetics of their new buildings. This is not surprising as almost every respondent worked in their library both pre- and post-construction so comparison between older and newer facilities is apparent and dramatic.

The Crump/Freund "Library User Survey" and "Library Staff Survey" proved valuable assessment tools and results reveal many parallel and consistent responses across the five libraries. The majority of respondents to the Crump-Freund "Library User Survey" (77 percent) were undergraduates. The first question that touches on library buildings asked the users "why do you usually come to the library?" Twenty reasons were listed for users to check if appropriate, including two that deal with physical desks found in the building, "check-out or renew a book" and "consult with a librarian." Assuming most users link consulting with librarians and checking out books as reference/ information desk activities, the overall percentage of users stating they come to a library to consult a librarian is shockingly low – 4 percent. Meanwhile, 37 percent of the composite users indicate they do visit a library to check-out or renew a book. These responses seem to indicate that service points for the circulation of materials and/or the availability of self-check-out equipment may continue to be a valued and utilized function. Ultimately, these survey responses may raise the question whether the traditional, physical "reference desk" remains a necessary element in a twenty-first century academic library building.

Another question from the Crump/Freund user survey regarding library space – "What do you think of the present library facility?"– contained a list of several building features for users to rate "yes" or "no." Across the five user groups the responses were remarkably similar and positive. Users answered positively for these elements:

- Location of service desks (97%)
- Safety and security (95%)
- Adequate staffing (94%)
- Cleanliness and inviting space (88%)
- Adequate space for collaborative study (73%)
- Adequate equipment (73%)
- Adequate space (72%)
- Adequate furniture (71%)
- Adequate space for individual study (70%).

Narrative comments from the Crump/Freund "Library User Survey" reveal more detail about specific features and conflict somewhat with the positive numerical ratings. Many problems with the new library buildings are chronicled by the narratives, with multiple users commenting negatively on several building features:

- Insufficient amount of available computer workstations
- Insufficient quantity of furniture – especially tables
- Insufficient quantity and quality of group study rooms
- Insufficient quantity of individual study spaces
- Poor layout/design of the building
- Insufficient quantity of electrical outlets
- Uncomfortable seating options
- Overcrowding at peak times
- Adverse noise levels
- Insufficient quantity quiet space
- Unclean appearance.

Additionally, a few users took the opportunity to mention "bad policies" of their library. While this last category is not necessarily building related, such feedback should be taken seriously by libraries striving to create a positive user experience. The Crump/Freund "Library Staff Survey" responses indicate staff perceives that users want their libraries to offer both quiet and collaborative spaces – and more of each – as well as additional computers and workstations.

Respondents to the Crump/Freund "Library Staff Survey" offer mostly positive responses with regard to new facilities. Four questions from the survey addressed library buildings and space, with one asking the staff to rate "yes" or "no" on the same nine questions (as the user survey) regarding their library facility. Staff offered similar high ratings for these elements:

- Location of service desks (80%)
- Safety and security (85%)
- Cleanliness and inviting space (72%)
- Adequate furniture (66%).

However, unlike the users' overwhelmingly positive responses to the other five categories, staff were more ambivalent in rating positively the following features:

- Adequate space for collaborative study (58%)
- Adequate space for individual study (53%)
- Adequate space (52%)
- Adequate equipment (50%)
- Adequate staffing (49%).

As with the narratives received from respondents to the user survey, staff comments flesh out many issues and problems that simple "yes" or "no" responses do not reveal. Several staff respondents commented negatively on insufficient space and seating in the library, particularly study space for both groups and individuals. Others commented about inadequate quantities of available computer workstations. Negative comments about service desks indicated that they were often poorly located. Additionally there were comments about inadequate housekeeping/ maintenance, inadequate staffing levels, and concerns about security.

Additional questions in the Crump/Freund staff survey elicited responses about their new buildings and post-occupancy concerns. Eighty-nine percent of respondents indicated that they worked in a facility that had undergone significant renovations in the past five years, while 17 percent worked in library building newly constructed in the last five years. Respondents were asked to rate 13 different features of their library with a response of "excellent," "above average," "satisfactory," "below average," or "poor." The following nine features received positive ("excellent," "above average," or "satisfactory" ratings from staff respondents (percentage of positive responses noted):

- Lighting (81%)
- Materials – floors, paint, etc. (83%)
- Overall environment (86%)
- Books/bound serials stacks (86%)
- Information commons (92%)
- Study space (72%)
- Circulation desk (90%)
- Reference desk (81%)
- Staff meeting rooms (80%).

Some features of library buildings received a majority negative rating ("below average," "poor") with overall percentages noted:

- General layout/building design (35% negative, 21% positive)
- Staff offices (31% negative, 22% positive)
- Elevators (31% negative, 25% positive)
- Work areas/office layout (35% negative, 15% positive).

While most respondents indicated their feelings about the features of their new or renovated buildings were mostly positive, some noticeable areas such as the basic design and layout of the building were received more negatively on average. Staff respondents indicated that meeting spaces were satisfactory, yet there were levels of dissatisfaction with regard to personal office space and the layout of the workspace.

Conclusion

Through a review of relevant literature, analysis of three related surveys, and several onsite visits to new library spaces and buildings, we have gleaned a number of trends and formulated some observations and recommendations for libraries launching renovations or new building projects.

Below are ten general observations about the library spaces now and in the future:

1. Libraries will need to continually reinvent their places and roles on academic campuses.
2. Library buildings will continue to be centers for the collection, access, and sharing of information, even as older print materials are moved increasingly to off-campus storage facilities.
3. Library buildings will continue to provide spaces for patron services.
4. Library buildings will continue to serve as meeting places and collaborative centers.
5. Space for quiet study is still valued.
6. Easy access to computing equipment is still a need on academic campuses.
7. Library patrons continue to check out physical materials for use elsewhere.
8. Library spaces will need to be continually adapted to accommodate changing technologies and user behaviors.

9. Remedies for spaces that are not functioning well, or not serving the changing needs of users, should be carefully considered for implementation.

10. If stationary, staffed reference service points are phased out, or less prominent, alternative modes of assistance should be implemented (roving staff, point-of-use signage, virtual reference services, and so on).

Below are five recommendations for the building design process:

1. During the design phase of a building project, input should be gathered from all stakeholders: administrators, librarians, front-line staff, and users.

2. Building materials and fixtures should be selected not only for their aesthetic value, but also taking into account durability and ease and cost of ongoing maintenance.

3. Well-designed, integrated signage is key. It should not be an afterthought.

4. Natural day lighting should be incorporated in the design where possible.

5. Flexibility is a virtue. Adaptable interior spaces and movable, modular furnishing allow users to self-configure spaces to serve different needs.

Lewis, in his 2007 *College & Research Libraries* article, points out that new library buildings are designed to "create comfortable, lively, and active spaces where students can interact with each other, with information and with technology and where support for the use of library resources and technology can be found" (p. 8). Libraries are maintaining their unique and relevant missions on academic campuses by expanding services and offering space that is more than just another study hall, a place to check out books, or alternative computing lab. A shift in focus in patron services can be observed when comparing the academic libraries of today with those of the past. Years ago users went to libraries primarily to access collections and find a quiet place for research and solitary study. While contemplative space is still needed and desired for some tasks, many users now seek out the library: a place to meet others, to collaborate with a group of friends or project partners, to hear a speaker, to use a meeting room, to access free wi-fi from their tablet or laptop, and even as a place to buy a cup of coffee or grab a quick snack.

If emphasis is increasingly placed on user activity over access to physical collections, particularly in the undergraduate setting, libraries must create spaces that are attractive, flexible, integrated with technology, intellectually stimulating, and that support communication and research. The library building must provide a functional, user-friendly environment or there won't be any users! Research conducted in preparation for this chapter has shown that new academic library buildings are being designed to welcome patrons with inviting areas for group study and conversation, while still providing comfortable spaces for computing, individual study, and research. The demand for more user space is driving the widespread practice for academic libraries to relocate substantial portions of their physical collections to off-campus storage facilities.

New building construction and renovation projects are complex and millions of dollars are involved, so all phases of the process must be carefully planned. As onsite visits and the surveys showed, problems with spaces and furnishings post-occupancy are frequently not addressed either because of expense or weariness following the construction phase. Administrators are hesitant to tinker with a building after a renovation has just been completed. This makes the design and implementation phases of a project even more crucial. The selection of an architect, construction managers, and contractors must be made carefully, and the librarians and staff along with administration should have ample opportunity to discuss their needs and desires before construction commences. It is also imperative for decision makers to gather information from a variety of sources, including the users. Georgia Tech Library canvassed undergraduates for feedback on renovation of their Learning Commons and created focus groups. Subsequently, their users offered substantial input to the design process of two projects. This kind of foresight produces a better product. It is, after all, the experienced librarians, staff, and users themselves who can provide keen insight on what design and space elements might best work – and not work – in a new or renovated library building.

References

ACRL. (2010). 2010 top ten trends in academic libraries: A review of the current literature. *College & Research Libraries News*, 71, 286–292.

Adhami, N. (2011). *Post-occupancy evaluation of Library West's interior design: A method to explore pre-design research and programming*. Gainesville, FL: University of Florida.

ALA. (2011). *ACRL/LLAMA guide for architects and librarians. Academic library building design: Resources for planning.* Retrieved from *http://wikis.ala.org/acrl/index.php/ACRL/LLAMA_Guide_for_Architects_and_Librarians*

Allen, F. R. (2011). The knowledge commons: Reasserting the library as the heart of campus. *College & Research Libraries News, 72,* 468–469.

ARL. (2009). *Innovative spaces in ARL libraries: Results of a 2008 study.* Retrieved from *http://www.arl.org/bm~doc/innovative-spaces-2009.pdf*

ASERL. (2000). *Shaping the future: ASERL's competencies for research libraries.* Retrieved from *http://www.aserl.org/programs/competencies/*

Barclay, D. A., & Scott, E. D. (2011). *The Library renovation, maintenance, and construction handbook.* New York: Neal-Schuman.

Bazillion, R. J., & Braun, C. (1995). *Academic libraries as high-tech gateways: A guide to design and space decisions.* Chicago: American Library Association.

Bennett, S. (2006). The choice for learning. *The Journal of Academic Librarianship, 32,* 3–13.

Bisbrouck, M., Desjardins, J., Menil, C., Ponce, F., & Rouyer-Gayett, F. (2004) *Libraries as places: Buildings for the 21st century.* Munchen: K. G. Saur.

Brown, C. R. (2002). *Interior design for libraries: Drawing on function and appeal.* Chicago: American Library Association.

Buschman, J. E., & Leckie, G. J. (2007). *The library as place.* Westport, CT: Libraries Unlimited.

CLIR. (2008). *No brief candle: Reconceiving research libraries for the 21st century.* Washington, DC: Council on Library and Information Resources.

Collins, B. (1999). *Building a scholarly communication center: Modeling the Rutgers experience.* Chicago: American Library Association.

Conley, C. (2006, 21 October). Libraries beckon, but stacks of books aren't part of pitch. *The Wall Street Journal.*

Dunlap, I. H. (1995). *CPR and the Library: Resuscitating the heart of the university.* Retrieved from *http://www.wiu.edu/users/mfihd/research/heart/heart.html*

Fox, R., & Stuart, C. (2009). Creating learning spaces through collaboration: How one library refined its approach. *EDUCAUSE Quarterly, 32.* Retrieved from *http://www.educause.edu/EDUCAUSE+Quarterly/EDUCAUSEQuarterly MagazineVolum/CreatingLearningSpacesThroughC/163850*

Grose, T. K. (2010, March). The place to go: Libraries reinvent themselves to serve digital-age students. *Prism: American Society for Engineering Education.* Retrieved from *http://www.prism-magazine.org/mar10/tt_01.cfm*

Harland, P. C. (2011). *The learning commons: Seven simple steps to transform your library.* Santa Barbara, CA: Libraries Unlimited.

Hassanain, M. A. & Mudhei, A. A. (2006). Post-occupancy evaluation of academic and research library facilities. *Structural Survey, 24*(3), 230–239. DOI: 10.1108/02630800610678878.

Kolowich, S. (2009, 6 November). Bookless libraries? *Inside Higher Ed.* Retrieved from *http://www.insidehighered.com/news/2009/11/06/library*

Kolowich, S. (2011). A truly bookless library. *Education Digest, 76,* 35–36.

Kusack, J. M. (1991). *Evaluating library buildings: Principles and procedures for post-occupancy evaluation.* Retrieved from *http://www.eric.ed.gov/ERICWebPortal/recordDetail?accno=ED374822*

Lackney, J. A., & Zajfen, P. (2005). Post-occupancy evaluation of public libraries: Lessons learned from three case studies. *Library Administration & Management, 19*(1), 16. Retrieved from *http://search.proquest.com/docview/216634217?accountid=10920*

Lewis, D. W. (2007). A strategy for academic libraries in the first quarter of the 21st century. *College & Research Libraries, 68*(5). Retrieved from *https://scholarworks.iupui.edu/bitstream/handle/1805/953/DWLewis_Strategy.pdf*

Lushington, N. (2002). *Libraries designed for users.* New York: Neal-Schuman.

Lynn, V. (2011). A knowledge commons needs assessment: Building for the future at Penn State. *College & Research Libraries News, 72,* 464–467.

McCarthy, R. C. (2007). *Managing your library construction project: A step-by-step guide.* Chicago: American Library Association.

Mullins, J. L., Allen, F. R., & Hufford, J. R. (2007). Top ten assumptions for the future of academic libraries and librarians: A report from the ACRL Research Committee. *College & Research Libraries News, 68,* 240–241.

Preiser W. F. E., & Wang, X. (2008). Quantitative (GIS) and qualitative (BPE) assessments of library performance. *Archnet-IJAR, 2*(1), 212–231. Retrieved from *http://archnet.org/gws/IJAR/8821/files_8181/2.1.10%20-w.preiser-x.wang-pp212-231.pdf*

Sannwald, W. W. (2001). *Checklist of library building design considerations.* Chicago: American Library Association.

Schallen, J. (Comp.). (n.d.). Practical tips for building design [post on the OCLC WebJunction discussion board]. Retrieved from *http://www.webjunction.org/documents/wj/Practical_Tips_for_Library_Building_Design.html*

Shill, H. B., & Tonner, S. (2004). Does the building still matter? Usage patterns in new, expanded, and renovated libraries, 1995–2002. *College & Research Libraries, 65*(2), 123–150.

Spencer, M. E. (2007). The state-of-the-art: NCSU Libraries Learning Commons. *Reference Services Review, 35,* 310–321.

Stewart, C. (2010). *The academic library building in the digital age: A study of construction, planning, and design of new library space.* Chicago: American Library Association.

Woodward, J. (2010). *Countdown to a new library: Managing the building project* (2nd ed.). Chicago: American Library Association.

Additional resources

ALA. (2012). *Building libraries and library additions: A selected annotated bibliography.* Retrieved from *http://www.ala.org/tools/libfactsheets/alalibraryfactsheet11*

American Libraries. (2008). 2008 library design showcase: The green scene. *American Libraries, 39*, 44–58.

Brophy, P. (2007). *The library in the 21st century*. London: Facet.

Florida State University. (n.d.). *Inside look: Strozier library renovations*. Retrieved from *http://www.fsu.com/Videos/News/Inside-look-Strozier-library-renovations*

Darnton, R. (2009). *The case for books: Past, present and future*. New York: PublicAffairs.

Freeman, G. T. (2005). *Library as place: Rethinking roles, rethinking space*. Washington, DC: Council on Library & Information Resources.

Freund, L., & Seale, C. (2007). Transforming Library West at the University of Florida: A fairy tale makeover. *Florida Libraries, 50*, 14–16.

Georgia Tech Library. (n.d.). The Commons at the Georgia Tech Library. Retrieved from *http://librarycommons.gatech.edu/*

Haas, L., & Robertson, J. (2004). *The information commons*. ARL SPEC Kit 281. Washington, DC: Association of Research Libraries, Office of Leadership and Management Services.

Lazzaro, J. (2001). *Adaptive technologies for learning & work environments*. Chicago: American Library Association.

Leighton, P. D. (1999). *Planning academic and research library buildings*. Chicago: American Library Association.

Loder, M. (2010). Libraries with a future: How are academic library usage and green demands changing building designs? *College & Research Libraries, 71*(4), 348–360.

Mash, S. D. (2010). *Decision making in the absence of certainty: A study in the context of technology and the construction of the 21st century academic library*. Chicago: American Library Association.

National Institute of Building Sciences. (2012). *Whole Building Design Guide (WBDG): Libraries*. Retrieved from *http://www.wbdg.org/design/libraries.php*

Primary Research Group. (2008). *Academic library building renovation benchmarks*. New York: Primary Research Group.

San Jose Mercury News. (2010, 18 May). Stanford University prepares for the "bookless library." *San Jose Mercury News*.

Schlipf, F. A., & Moorman, J. (2011). *The Seven Deadly Sins of public library architecture*. Retrieved from *http://www.urbanafreelibrary.org/about/affiliations/presentations/sevensins/sevensins.pdf*

Trotter, D. W. (2008). Going for the green. *American Libraries, 39*, 40–43.

University of Central Florida Libraries. (2010). *University libraries knowledge commons – fall 2010*. Retrieved from *http://library.ucf.edu/NewLook/Default.php*

UNC Health Sciences Library. (2012). *Collaboration*. Retrieved from *http://www.hsl.unc.edu/Collaboration/index.cfm*

Webb, T. D. (2000). *Building libraries for the 21st century: The shape of information*. Jefferson, NC: McFarland.

Williamsburg Regional Library. (2001). *Library construction from a staff perspective*. Jefferson, NC: McFarland & Co.

Wilsted, T. P. (2007). *Planning new and remodeled archival facilities*. Chicago: American Library Association.

Appendix

New Library Spaces: Post-Occupancy Survey

Has your library been renovated or newly constructed in the past five years? If so, please consider filling out a short questionnaire (ten questions) focused on gauging staff satisfaction on various elements of the design and functionality of the new building or renovated space.

Where do you work?
Institution:
Library (e.g. Main, Branch, etc.):
Department:
What is your position (e.g. reference librarian) in the library?

1. What building or space was renovated or recently built? (check all that apply)

2. What building or space was renovated or recently built? (check all that apply)

   – Main library building

   – Information commons

   – Reference/Circulation area(s)

   – Branch library/Public space

   – Staff areas

   – Other (please list building/space):

3. How many years have you worked in the library before and after the renovation or new building was erected?

   – Before construction

   – After construction

4. Did staff have input during the planning and design stages of the renovated space or new building?

   – Yes

   – No

   – Comment:

5. Did staff have input on features that worked or needed adjusting after the renovation or new building was opened?

  – Yes

  – No

  – Comment:

6. Please rate the following physical features of the library:

Very dissatisfied Moderately dissatisfied Neither dissatisfied or satisfied Moderately satisfied Very satisfied

(a) Location of Staff offices and meeting rooms

(b) Location and amount of user/study space

(c) Amount of collaborative space created

(d) Windows and natural lighting

(e) Amount of stack space made available

(f) Artificial and task lighting

(g) Noise levels in offices/workspaces

(h) Noise levels in user/study spaces

(i) Stacks and storage arrangement

(j) General design and floor plans

(k) Placement of reference/info desks

7. Please rate the following functional features of the library:

Very dissatisfied Moderately dissatisfied Neither dissatisfied or satisfied Moderately satisfied Very satisfied

(a) Traffic/workflows in offices/workspaces

(b) Security of offices/workspaces

(c) Security of user/study spaces

(d) Level of ADA compliancy

(e) Layout of the offices/workspaces in your department

(f) Furniture supplied in your offices/workspaces

(g) Furniture supplied in the user/study spaces

8. Please rate the following aesthetic and psychological features of the library:

Very dissatisfied Moderately dissatisfied Neither dissatisfied or satisfied Moderately satisfied Very satisfied

(a) Comfort level and ambiance

(b) Materials used in the building

(c) Color and brightness

(d) Attractiveness of design

(e) Privacy in offices/workspaces

(f) Privacy in user/study spaces

(g) Building temperature and ventilation

9. What features could be improved in your renovated or new library building?

10. What features could be improved in your renovated or new library building?

   – Other comments?

4

Assess to cultivate your own library

Michele J. Crump

Abstract: Measuring the value of the library in the academic community, and the value of library resources and services to its customer remains a critical topic in libraries, primarily because of the downturn in the economy and the rising cost of education. This chapter reviews selected practices for assessment evaluations, anthropological and ethnographic studies, trend monitoring, and user experience in academic libraries. The surveys and studies discussed by the author propose methods for achieving pertinent services through assessment endeavors, which characterize student and faculty users' preferences.

Key words: library anthropological studies, library assessment, library ethnographic studies, library service, library trends, user experience in libraries, user feedback, user survey.

"We need to learn from each other. You cannot, of course, lift one way of doing things, transplant it to the other side of the earth and expect it to flourish."

– H. McRae (2010) *What works: Success in stressful times*, p. xxii

"Today, librarians face a new assessment challenge: to articulate the value of academic libraries within an institutional context."

– M. Oakleaf (2011) Are they learning? Are we? Learning outcomes and the academic library, p. 77

Introduction

In the previous chapter, Carrico and Lindell examined the physical structure of the library information commons (IC), and discussed how interior design defines the place where students participate in academic activities. The facilities built or renovated in recent years to accommodate an information/learning commons are successful when the assessments and planning have included input from administrators, librarians, and library customers. As Carrico and Lindell note, post-occupancy assessments are essential to ensuring that the new setting enriches services and advances the complete research experience for users.

Assessment in academic libraries may take many forms, but the end results if applied thoughtfully should renew services and demonstrate the value of the library to its parent institution. In this chapter the author examines library assessment practices that resonate with the perceptions outlined in Chapter 1. The effective methodology highlighted in the following studies do not recommend cookie-cutter approaches that librarians could simply put in place – instead the studies suggest that they observe and assess their own environment to gauge the needs and desires of their clientele so that customer-based services can be established. Through interviews with users and some self-reflection, the librarians conducting these studies connected with students and faculty in a tangible way and discovered their customers' critical perceptions about behavior, service, and communication. Librarians now know that engaging in customer outreach is an essential element for bridging the divide and encouraging collaborative relationships in the academic environment. Accordingly, librarians and educators committed to forming communities within the library and at their institutions are applying these reflective methods to overcome assumptions and cultivate learning (Oakleaf, 2011, p. 72).

Surveys tracking trends and perceptions

In this section the author examines educational environment scans with an emphasis on emerging technologies and educational practices that may influence the way library users approach research. It also reviews standard library service evaluations, which query library users' satisfaction with services, resources, and the library as place. The instrumental surveys included consider specifically the academic arena in evaluating faculty and librarian reactions to technical innovation as it changes the way the professionals teach, research, and interact with students. The following tools offer a good foundation for exploring current and future thinking about the educational landscape. Keeping up or staying ahead of developments is simply not possible but responsible educators and librarians make the attempt because they want to understand the world their students encounter and be ready to respond to their frustrations with empathy and courtesy.

The EDUCAUSE Center for Applied Research (ECAR) performs an influential survey annually that analyzes undergraduates' usage of technology. Since 2004, their *National Study of Undergraduate Students and Information Technology* has tracked ownership and usage trends in technology to project how teachers and students might adapt and apply emerging tools in education. The 2011 survey report garnered information "from a nationally representative sample of 3,000 students in 1,179 colleges and universities" (Dahlstrom, deBoor, Grunwald, & Vockley, 2011, p. 33). On the whole, students seem comfortable with technology. Indeed, the survey findings show that, "More than half feel they know more about technology than their instructors, and many of the technologies that professors use effectively are nevertheless ones students still wish they would use more often"(Dahlstrom et al., 2011, p. 5). The savvy confidence recorded here validates the view that students, whether true or not, believe they have the advantage over librarians and faculty when it comes to applying technology in their academic work and social communications. The ECAR findings state that students want their teachers to use technology more often because it makes learning an immersive, engaging, and relevant experience, which explains why students value learning when teachers incorporate some online instruction (Dahlstrom et al., 2011, p. 6).

Underlining student preference for classroom technology, the ECAR 2011 report shows that 57 percent of students surveyed use e-books or e-textbooks and prefer this technology especially for text-books, which when available in digital format are usually less expensive (Dahlstrom et al., 2011, p. 14). The movement toward increased usage in digital monographs upholds library collection purchasing shifts from print to digitalized formats. However, only 24 percent are accessing library digital resources from their smartphones (Dahlstrom et al., 2011, p. 15). With the development of portable tablets and mini-laptops, the authors wonder if using the smartphone for quick and especially lengthy information access will decrease even further with the publication of the next year's ECAR report. These smaller mobile laptops seem destined to change the way students engage in learning. The clear directive gleaned from these longitudinal findings is that educators who become familiar with the technology students use for communicating, entertainment, and social networking may want to "create an action plan to better integrate technology into courses and help students access institutional and academic information from their many and diverse devices and platforms"

(Dahlstom et al., 2011, p. 32) – a resounding missive for academic librarians as well.

The Horizon Report published annually since 2005, is a collaborative effort of the New Media Consortium and the EDUCAUSE Learning Initiative (Johnson, Smith, Willis, Levine, & Haywood, 2011). The report offers a heads-up analysis of "emerging technologies likely to have a large impact over the coming five years on a variety of sectors around the globe" (Johnson et al., 2011, p. 2). In identifying the technology influencing activities of students and educators alike, the report describes how these emerging tools persist and contribute to high expectations concerning immediate access and user-centered services. In addition to naming technology trends to monitor, the report ranks the most influential technologies and forecasts an implementation timeframe for each. The top four "near term" trends named in the 2011 report are repeats from the 2010 report: electronic books, mobile technology, augmented reality, and game-based learning (Johnson et al., 2011, pp. 12, 16, 20). These trends reinforce the collaborative, mobile, hyper-connected, and hyper-active environment in which we all live. In particular, students anticipate ease of access to the "abundance of resources" available "outside of the formal campus" (Johnson et al., 2011, p. 3) from anywhere at any time and want their educational experiences to be fully participatory. The benefit of scanning this prognostic report every year is the insight it provides concerning the landscape of education – where it is headed and what librarians can do to realize programs that will appropriately address students' and teachers' learning expectations.

The author cannot talk about library assessment without acknowledging Association of Research Library's (ARL) ARL Statistics, LibQUAL+®, and now LibQUAL+® Lite quantitative and qualitative measurement products. While ARL Statistics measure the growth of collections, staff, expenditures and transactions for some services, LibQUAL+® has become the standard bearer for measuring "user satisfaction and measures of service effectiveness" (Forrest, 2009, p. 9). The development and fine tuning of the LibQUAL+® longitudinal surveys is thoroughly covered in the literature and much of it is available online from ARL. The surveys canvass library users' preferences and opinions about "effect of service, reliability, library as place, provision of physical collections, and access to collections" (Waller & Hipps, 2002, p. 10). In practice, implementing and analyzing the results proficiently require library and library staff commitment and involvement "in qualitative and quantitative research methods and working assessment activities into their plans and budgets" (Waller & Hipps, 2002, p. 10). Simply put, the tool if used effectively could contribute resourceful means for describing how the library participates in the research mission of its parent institution. As well, if applied annually or biennially as ARL suggests, the tool advances the analytical skills of library staff and fosters a culture of assessment within the library and in the academic community (ARL, 2012).

With the introduction of LibQUAL+® Lite in 2010, ARL seeks to improve response time through an item question sampling method that reduces the number of questions patrons are asked (Thompson, Kyrillidou, & Cook, 2012). Even with this shorter iteration of the survey, the time commitment and analytical skills required to extract and present the user feedback still tax library staff's abilities to apply the findings in a meaningful way (ARL, 2012). ARL frequently offers training sessions for conducting and interpreting LibQUAL+® survey results in its effort to form a worldwide community of assessment (ARL, 2012). Repeated use of the instrument and broad marketing campaigns that pronounce the benefits of this educational experience could raise user, staff, and faculty "buy in" so that participants become active and willing partners in the assessment activity (Waller& Hipps, 2002). Early adopters of LibQUAL+®, those libraries that made using the survey tool a priority, may be ahead of the game because they have acquired reliable measurements that gauge the quality of their library services over time and validate decisions librarians make for introducing value-added services.

Training time and the complexity of analyzing results might explain why some libraries have developed brief "quick and dirty" or homegrown evaluative instruments to capture user perceptions in a more judicious/ practical way. As libraries are asked by their institutions to prove their value, ongoing reliable and tested assessment will certainly become expected practice. Recent library position postings show an expansion in new librarian jobs devoted to assessment and qualitative evaluation efforts. Librarians in these leadership roles will be called upon to direct user-based studies that inform learning and service goals, and will proactively work with library staff to form an environment of evaluation.

Two surveys that Ithaka S+R conducts periodically concerning faculty and library directors' perceptions correspond to the student and librarian surveys discussed later in this chapter. The 2009 faculty survey shows that 90 percent of faculty believe that the library should focus on building collections to support their research (Schonfeld, 2010, p. 9). Continuing with the collection theme, 71 percent of faculty viewed the library as an archive and only 59 percent as a portal to electronic resources (Schonfeld, 2010, p. 9). Using the services of librarians for research support ranked at 51 percent for faculty but only 45 percent expect teaching support from librarians (Schonfeld, 2010, p. 10). Because faculty view collection development as a critical library function, proactive librarians might take advantage of this positive perception and begin building rapport with faculty by asking them for input on selection decisions important to their research and teaching interests.

The Ithaka S+R library survey report indicates that 94 percent of the directors surveyed "see teaching information literacy skills to undergraduates as a very important role for libraries" (Long & Schonfeld, 2010, p. 27). This viewpoint directly opposes the perceptions expressed by faculty. As with students, it seems that faculty are acquiring and filling research needs by using a variety of search engines to access scholarly information instead of beginning their research at the library web page or catalog. In fact, the faculty survey reports that, "only 21 percent of respondents reported that they began their research process at either the library building or the library's online catalog" (Long & Schonfeld, 2010, p. 25). When compared, the two surveys identify a perception gap between faculty and library administrators. Faculty focus on collection and library directors are more concerned with services that support research and teaching (Long & Schonfeld, 2010). Clearly, librarians need to find a way to change faculty perceptions about their instruction role. In order to shape partnerships, teaching faculty, deans, and library deans/directors should work together to form well-defined directives, whether in mission statements or teaching objectives, that show commitment to developing programs in the classroom and the library for strengthening students' information literacy skills.

The captivating studies in the next section center on campus-based investigations of student and faculty research practices and technology usage through survey methods or anthropological and ethnographical evaluations.

Anthropological and ethnographic approaches to assessment

Often big changes in a library organization present an opportunity to introduce innovative thinking. The University of Florida went through a major renovation of its Humanities and Social Science collections library, Library West, in 2004–06. At the time, IC were being put in place in many academic libraries but anthropological library studies were not a hot trend. The focus of the day was on bringing technology into the library to increase access to and knowledge of the growing digital collections. The library took advantage of this renovation opportunity to develop a plan for a collaborative reference and technology area in Library West that would offer students the complete research experience. The Info Commons Concept Team, comprised of librarians from service areas within Library West and other branch libraries, was charged with exploring other facilities and identifying methods for gathering customer input about design and services in the area (Cataldo, Freund, Ochoa, & Salcedo, 2006, p. 25). The assessment this team directed included site visits to other academic library facilities, surveys of faculty and students, and focus groups (Cataldo et al., 2006, pp. 29–32). A participatory workshop hosted by the School of Art and Art History invited students to use their imaginations in designing their vision of the ideal library. The California design consultant who led the student group activities made an impression on the Concept Team, who also participated in the workshop. Some of the more original and customer-based ideas generated in the brainstorming session were included in the final implementation of services, furnishings, and facility layout (Cataldo et al., 2006, pp. 44–6).

As a precursor to the assessments that follow, the IC Concept Team had great hopes for this implementation to serve as a hub for student and librarian research instruction and collaboration (Cataldo et al., 2006, p. 38). The area is heavily used for students collaborating with each other, making use of many available desktop computers and supporting software to produce inventive projects; however, reference librarians are not included in this hubbub of creativity. What is not working? The following anthropological studies and investigative surveys interview students and observe their behaviors as they perform research and use technology in the library.

The ground-breaking undergraduate student study the University of Rochester conducted to "guide the libraries' efforts to improve library facilities, reference outreach and the libraries' Web presence" and address the question, "What do students really do when they write their research papers?" established an anthropological and ethnographic approach to surveying library users (Gibbons & Foster, 2007, p. v). Focusing on the research habits and processes of undergraduates at their institution, the Undergraduate Research Project over a two-year span engaged 35 library staff and many undergraduates and employed anthropological methods such as interviews, focus groups, usability testing, photography surveys, and mapping diaries to gain student, faculty and library staff input about library services and design (Gibbons & Foster, 2007). Nancy Fried Foster, the anthropologist of the study, profiles reference librarians at University of Rochester, River Campus Libraries, illustrating how their roles have changed as undergraduates under-utilize available library services. The print collection and the librarians' subject expertise are undervalued because students are not seeking the help of the reference librarian as they have in the past. Internet search engines are much more convenient, easy to use and available 24/7 from students' various technologies. Foster notes that the librarians' function acts as a true motivation for the study – "the desire to figure out what it would take to get more students to come to the desk asking for help, to restore the face-to-face interactions and the opportunities to provide that special kind of service – caring and personalized, intellectually demanding, expert and informed – that attracted so many librarians to their field in the first place" (Foster, 2007, p. 72). The allure and self-service features of technology have usurped personalized service – how do librarians get that service prospect back, or do they?

It is difficult to regain the customers' trust and confidence when the customer does not understand the range and complexity of librarianship. To the student every service desk is there for the same purpose and every person behind that desk is a clerk or librarian. Foster examines the contrasting models of service that are held by the student and the librarian. Her anthropological analysis reveals very different prototypes – the librarians' full-service model as opposed to the students' self-service model (Foster, 2007, p. 75). Indeed, the "big box" library buildings that have become prevalent on university campuses reinforce the idea of self-service with large areas and movable furniture that students can arrange to suit their individual or group study needs. When they need help, they go to the first available desk because they do not have a clear concept of what a reference librarian does. The library as place for the user seems to trump library and librarian as content provider.

If "self-service is the preeminent model" (Foster, 2007, p. 76), then convenience is surely foremost in the student's perception about seeking a librarian's help in the library. Foster suggests that a single service point staffed with a mixture of student worker, staff and librarians might attract students (Foster, 2007, p. 77). She is not advocating that academic libraries respond to all the expectations undergraduates might have concerning their library experience; rather, she thinks that librarians should be partnering with faculty because students seem to value the opinion of their teachers and their parents almost exclusively when it comes to research assignments (Foster, 2007, p. 77).

This study also exposed to the surprise of the researchers that "students are on average no more proficient with computer technology than librarians or faculty members" (Gibbons & Foster, 2007, p. 81). Slowly, but we hope surely, librarians are coming to realize that the online catalog, electronic resource databases, and even the library website is often too complex and confusing for library users, which in turn inhibits ease of access to scholarly resources. The full focus of providing user-centered services should above all simplify access: "We might not want our students to use Google all the time, but giving them Google-like simplicity in the library interface – on top of functionality that supports precision searching and advanced forms of browsing – would certainly be desirable" (Foster, 2007, p. 77).

A key outcome of this project shows that library staff have become more experimental in their approach to trying new service ideas (Gibbons & Foster, 2007, p. 82). The "nimble" (McRae, 2010, p. x) factor has finally become a reality with library staff as they feel free to experiment without the fear of failure or the need for committees to bless the experimenting (Gibbons & Foster, 2007, p. 82). In turn, the librarians at the University of Rochester have a more open relationship with students and seeking their input is becoming the norm (Gibbons & Foster, 2007, p. 82). The authors caution librarians ready to engage in new user-center services to consider their students – "socioeconomic conditions, the ratio of residential to commuter, local climate, and the robustness of the campus IT infrastructure" (Gibbons & Foster, 2007, p. 83) – before developing services that do not address the true needs of students.

Similar to the University of Florida's experience, the library study at Fresno State used the opportunities created by a library renovation project and an incoming dean to develop an anthropological library design and conduct an ethnographic study of student life on its campus (Delacore, Mullooly, & Scroggins, 2009, p. 9). Inspired by the work of Gibbons and Foster, the research team used similar methods of engaging students in interviews, surveys, mapping exercises, design exercises, and web usability/ design sessions but based their study in design anthropology methodology, which embraces users "in their natural contexts to deliver design insights that make for products and services that better meet users' needs and deliver a richer user experience" (Delacore et al., 2009, p. 6). The project acknowledges the diversity of its students and makes the reader aware of the various activities that make up student life today. The two anthropologists at Fresno State, leading a team of student helpers, mapped the student life of their public university to then revise user services in the refurbished Henry Madden Library (Delacore et al., 2009, p. 9).

Insights that emerged from this study mirror findings found in Gibbons and Fosters' (2007) report, but this study offers more insight into the complex lives of students when off the campus. Unlike the University of Rochester with its predominantly white student body that resides on campus, Fresno State has over 20 000 undergraduates, many of whom are first-generation college attendees (Delacore et al., 2009, p. 5). This highly diverse population often commutes to campus, attending school part-time because they more than likely have a full or part-time job (Delacore et al., 2009, p. 5). The Fresno State Library Study invited design students to participate in workshops in which they developed their ideas about library space and how it should be used. The students designed rooms that speak to "the whole of student life" (Delacore et al., 2009, p. 53), encompassing personal and customizable features and services to accommodate their varied student hours and their understanding of library. Something as simple as changing the signage from "Reference Desk" to "Ask Here" or "Need Help" (Delacore et al., 2009, p. 54) was more meaningful and inviting to these busy Fresno State library users.

The Ethnographic Research in Illinois Academic Libraries (ERIAL) Project includes five Illinois university libraries (Northeastern Illinois University, DePaul University, Illinois Wesleyan University, University of Illinois at Chicago, and University of Illinois at Springfield) and updates some of the notions put forth in the University of Rochester study. The five ERIAL teams interviewed teaching faculty and librarians, and evaluated undergraduate students' complete research practice, indicating that this unique approach makes this study the broadest in scope of the anthropological library inquiries (Asher, Miller, & Green, 2012, p. 2). ERIAL created a holistic view of students' perceptions about the educational process through examining their relationships with teaching faculty and librarians, assessing the role of the library and librarians in that process, and analyzing their findings to adjust services (Armstrong, 2012, p. 33). In the end they were able to make some general observations about undergraduate students as a whole but were cognizant of the unique student cultures on each campus that would inform distinct library services on their campuses.

Overall, ERIAL found that undergraduates did not have a good understanding of the librarians' role or how they might help them with class assignments. It is a little disheartening to read the ERIAL study results and realize the Illinois students some four years after the University of Rochester study are still arriving on campus "with an inability to discern between various types of sources and identify reliable and high-quality research materials" (Armstrong, 2012, p. 34). On these campuses, teaching faculty have perceived the lack of information literacy skills as a teaching/training issue and do offer some level of library instruction either in the classroom, at the library, or in one-on-one sessions (Armstrong, 2012, p. 37). However, the interviews with teaching faculty revealed that they too have observed that students really do not understand what the library is and believe that librarians need to "focus their energies on inserting themselves and the library into the general orientation process on their campuses" (Armstrong, 2012, p. 39). In order that students retain and understand how to navigate within the library, we would add to their recommendation that librarians instruct students about the basics of the library in straightforward language, devoid of any library terminology.

From this study and that of Gibbons and Foster, librarians are keenly aware that students might come to the library for supporting research information but will probably not seek a librarian's help in locating scholarly articles in databases or in organizing a search strategy (Duke, 2012, p. 145). The most effective way to turn this situation around according to the ERIAL teams is to build viable working relationships with faculty and thus become less invisible to students (Asher & Duke, 2012, p. 163). Their faculty interview results reinforce the assertions that Gibbons and Foster made about the positive supportive rapport students have with the teaching faculty. Student and faculty relationships are working. Now it is time for librarians to proactively demonstrate to students and teaching faculty how library "services and resources can benefit their immediate and long-term educational goals" (Duke & Asher, 2012, p. 167). However, two issues require librarians' close attention: students' perception of librarians and teaching faculty's reluctance to partner with librarians in building information literacy skills programs. Students see librarians as authority figures according to interviewed faculty but are reluctant to approach them because they seem too busy and appear forbidding (Armstrong, 2012, p. 38). We know from the ERIAL study that teaching faculty has developed empathetic relationships with their students. Following that lead, librarians should use every opportunity to show compassion and concern when assisting students, making their service experience a genuine encounter that they will likely want to repeat. The faculty–librarian relationship requires thoughtful leadership from all concerned as "there is no single action, or linear series of steps" (Armstrong, 2012, p. 47) to realize this necessary connection. Instead of seeing this as a daunting challenge, we think that librarians are in a position to create their professional futures as they build collaborative alliances with colleagues and teaching faculty to become rooted in the information literacy efforts of the academic community.

Brigham Young University library achieved a collaborative initiative with an Applied Anthropology class in their library ethnographic study of library use. The library hired undergraduate anthropology students to interview students about their research process (Washburn & Bibb, 2011, p. 58). We have to admire the creativity of this win–win partnership as the students gained valuable practical research experience while granting the library reliable and affordable interviewers to perform the research. Their anthropological study tested the "hypothesis regarding the use of students to study students" (Washburn & Bibb, 2011, p. 64). With the "short-term or rapid assessment" (Washburn & Bibb, 2011, p. 64) process they designed and the employment of a large number of students, the data could be collected, analyzed in an efficient timeframe. The Brigham Young model is an exceptional example of a partnership that reaches across the academic community. Students interviewing students might produce more genuine insights into the research practices of students within the library. One observation that would benefit any library considering the student interviewing student model would be to also involve the anthropology students in the development of the survey questions so that they have a sense of ownership and feel more comfortable with the survey instrument (Washburn & Bibb, 2011, p. 64).

The above studies touched on students' use of technology but Char Booth's (2009) compelling look at Ohio University students' use of Internet and emerging technologies reveals more about their specific technological skills and knowledge. Booth contributes a detailed analysis of student demographics and examines what technology tools students have integrated into their research methods. She engages us with her frank discussion about how many librarians rushed to adopt emerging technologies only to be disappointed because students failed to accept them in the library environment. Booth tests assumptions about students' technological skills against predetermined user traits pulled from popular generational classification schemes (Booth, 2009, p. 3). In addition she recognizes her "technolust" (Stephens, 2008, p. 314) and manages an objective and thorough environmental scan of the Ohio University students to gain real knowledge of their technology use and desires.

The scan results show that younger undergraduate students may "own and use more mobile and social tools, but they have not necessarily reached the stage in their academic development that allows them to see their value in a research context" (Booth, 2009, p. 102). Conversely, older students may not have all the new mobile devices but "are clearly more receptive to the idea of using various technologies in library context" (Booth, 2009, p. 94). To inform adoption and implementation of emerging technology, Booth used a locally developed web-based survey to find out what kinds of technology students are using currently and what they might use if the tool was implemented in the library environment. Booth underlines the need for defining local clientele through frequent assessment "in order to inform an ongoing cycle of innovation" (2009, p. 102). The sample survey she provides in the appendix is a modified version of the two-part instrument she used for the Ohio University study. Though lengthy, the survey is a good model for any library to customize and use on their campus for gauging the technology adoption of their students.

Rochester, Fresno State, ERIAL, Brigham Young, and Ohio University studies all point to the revelation that generalizations about students on one academic campus should not be applied to another without making adjustments that represent a "nuanced understanding of the daily lives of their students" (Asher & Duke, 2012, p. 161). Knowing students' socioeconomic background and their research behavior is essential in addressing the gap between librarian and student and will influence the services and resources that will be used. Some general observations that resonate in these studies may be viewed as warnings or wake-up calls to academic libraries: undergraduate students have replaced librarians with the Internet; the library is now a social place for interacting with other students but not with librarians; librarians need to develop working relationships with faculty. To address these issues, librarians must create new models for services and persistently monitor educational trends "to actively seek ways to engage more deeply in the academic community" (Asher & Duke, 2012, p. 167). As well, librarians must exercise quick-thinking, taking action promptly as scholastic requirements and technology evolve. Above all else, librarians need to change the perception students have about them and come out from behind the desk to offer user-friendly help with their research endeavors.

User experience in academic libraries

How can librarians transform their forbidding image and become more inviting and welcoming to library users? As with the anthropological studies, academic librarians often look outside library-centric models to adopt organizational or management prototypes for refining operations. Like the studies above, user experience (UX) is one such trend, which emanates from the web design community and has become a model for librarians concerned with enriching user services. There are many articles and blogs authored by public and university librarians that offer helpful advice on incorporating UX practices when developing user-centered services in libraries. Aaron Schmidt's (2010) UX column in *Library Journal*, launched on 1 January 2010, takes a direct approach to explaining what UX is and how the elements of user design can be applied to improve library services (pp. 28–29). Schmidt (2010) explains that librarians should be listening and observing their users "to develop an empathetic focus on people"(p. 29). Not unlike the techniques used in the anthropological and ethnographic studies, UX applies a holistic approach to problem-solving service issues and proactively involves customers before making service adjustments that will change their library experience (Fox & Doshi, 2011, p. 12).

Schmidt (2010) suggests that performing interviews with users rather than subjecting them to surveys will accomplish more unaffected and useful responses (p. 24). Identifying problems and recruiting interviewees to engage in face-to-face conversations brings the customer into the process, builds trust and may have very positive outcomes for future services (Schmidt, 2010, p. 24). He warns librarians about trying to impose a quick fix such as simply hiring a User Experience Librarian without investing in customer-based services in your library: "User experience isn't something that can be sprinkled onto a library to make it relevant and engaging to its users. To have a meaningful impact, user experience thinking must be integrated into all aspects of a library" (Schmidt, 2011, p. 24). Changing the culture and communication structure must take place with every library staff member taking responsibility for their role in fostering customer relationships to build trust and invite a reliable welcoming service.

Stephen Bell's blog *Designing Better Libraries* keeps the conversation about user experience alive with current posts relating to UX in the library environment. In an insightful post, Bell (2011) shares his contribution to the book *Listening to the Customer*, in which he urges library staff to have their "antennae up" for "breakthrough ideas" by listening and observing library users in the library. In addition, he directs librarians to be more involved in formal listening experiences such as: faculty and student library advisory groups, visits to department chairs, social networks, as well as surveys and focus groups. One intriguing idea Bell (2011) suggests is spending time walking around the library talking with students and engaging them in impromptu conversations in which they can express opinions about library space and service prospects. In other words, listening on all levels at every opportunity will serve the library well to be in touch with their customers' ideas, concerns and ensure an inviting/welcoming environment. Simply engaging with students helps to build their confidence in librarians' knowledge about resources and shows what librarians can do for them on a very real level.

The ARL SPEC Kit *Library User Experience* survey brings together UX activities that 71 out of 126 ARL member libraries are practicing currently, and serves as an admirable overview for designing and sustaining an essential customer experience within academic libraries (Fox & Doshi, 2011, p. 12). UX is an all-inclusive assessment methodology that encompasses user feedback, outreach to users, and commitment to cultivating flexible models for continued assessment (Fox & Doshi, 2011, p. 11). The SPEC Kit presents examples of practical application and suggests establishing standards for user-experience assessment in academic libraries. Fox and Doshi (2011) tell us that their collected data illustrates that user experience already has a broad interpretation within ARL libraries and can include "assessment, user engagement, library design, outreach, and marketing" (p. 11) as well as web usability testing. Currently in its infancy in academic libraries, we expect that UX standards and methodology will mature as librarians continue experimenting and adapting tools that become core features to the user experience in the library environment.

The authors share survey findings that reveal the types of assessment tools some of these ARL libraries are performing on a regular basis. For instance, many of the respondents conduct ARL LibQUAL+® surveys every two to three years but seem to prefer local survey type tools to readily assess students through anecdotal comment, focus groups, and usability testing (Fox & Doshi, 2011, p. 12). Forty-three percent of the libraries used incentives such as food or gift cards and noted that the feedback initiated inclusive redesign or some modification to library services or spaces, while 39 percent reported making minor adjustments to services (Fox & Doshi, 2011, p. 12). Ninety percent of the libraries share feedback results with their users and market the initiated changes resulting from feedback to their academic community (Fox & Doshi, 2011, p. 12). Overall, most respondents conduct assessment activities periodically but do not have a formal evaluation structure in place; thus, assessment becomes an "ad hoc" activity performed "by one or more units" (Fox & Doshi, 2011, p. 12). The authors suggest that one means for sustaining input from the library clientele is to establish library advisory boards. Eighty percent of the ARL library participants have an active library advisory board with members from teaching faculty and library staff (Fox & Doshi, 2011, p. 14). Fox and Doshi (2011) advocate that libraries truly commit to student engagement in UX activities by developing advisory broads with only student members (p. 14).

The studies examined here confirm that periodically surveying students, faculty, and other library users is not adequate. Employing a variety of assessment tools will help to extend diversity, sustainability, and reduce participant survey burnout (Fox & Doshi, 2011, p. 60). To stress the institutional commitment necessary for lasting assessment activities, Fox and Doshi include several job descriptions from the participants that exhibit leadership assignments indicative of the growing interest in assessment and UX in ARL libraries. These positions demonstrate the development and expressed need for proactive programs that will forge ongoing assessment to track technological innovations and evaluate users' application of technology (Fox & Doshi, 2011, pp. 186–193). Based on comments from survey participants, they expect a "future upward trend for these types of positions" (Fox & Doshi, 2011, p. 13) and believe that more academic libraries will begin including assessment and UX models in their strategic plans.

This SPEC Kit contributes to the body of growing UX library experiences, displaying applicable models already in place that are working well in bringing user experience to the academic library. User experience in academic libraries encompasses a wide range of assessment activities, which will become refined as the profession embraces this customer-based methodology and commits to sustainable models of assessment. Along with the SPEC Kit publication, devoted columns in library journals and blogs offer practical applications and go beyond simply sharing best practices but launch conversations about UX innovative techniques as they develop. We see glimmers of agility and flexibility in the models these columnists and bloggers share. With their urging and prodding, librarians are learning to listen and connect with library customers. Only time will tell if the UX direct approach to service will address the needs of library users arriving with different skills and higher expectations each year.

Conclusion

The studies reviewed in this chapter contribute evaluative tools and assessment practices to bring about substantive change in the services libraries offer their users. Such inventive approaches to measuring library services acknowledge a focus shift in library operations from collection-centric to customer-based services. The feedback process functions as a catalyst to adjust services but more importantly it offers insight into user perceptions about the library and librarians. The authors believe that making informed decisions that are grounded in the customer reduces the impulse to make assumptions, and produces service changes that effectively improve the research experience for the library user. Throughout the literature reviewed here, the researchers, primarily librarians, restate that the demographics for every institution are unique; thus, best practices or assessment examples will have a very different execution as models are tailored to fit the distinctive characteristics of each academic community. Emerging approaches to evaluating students and their library research practices show promise for guiding library services that will unite the library with its academic community mission.

Are librarians making progress with library assessment? Yes, but they must accelerate the progress by inviting students, faculty and library staff into the change process and begin communicating with their colleagues like never before. In a 2006 article about matrix teams this author explored the structure as a means for bridging communication across division lines to successfully bring about change and develop community within the library. Sadly, the bridge is incomplete. From top down and from one department to another, communication problems persist in library organizations and hinder progress. One thing stands out about the assessments examined in this chapter – projects succeed when administrators and library staff conceive a clear vision with well-defined objectives. Projects that bring library staff together to transform services that connect with students and faculty will "humanize library operations and empower library staff to think collegially about managing change and to think creatively about using technology" (Crump, 2006, p. 215). Librarians will continue having conversations that lead to collaboration within the library and reach across the divide to form relationships with students and faculty – the beginning of necessary community.

In the next chapter, Pascal Lupien and Randy Oldham discuss their longitudinal studies of emerging technology and the users' response to employing these tools in the library environment. Similar to Char Booth's analysis, Lupien and Oldham examine some assumptions that have been made in generational terms about students and their rapport with technology. Their eye-opening study tracks how students have used technology over time and may influence the way librarians implement and introduce technology to users at their institutions. As you read through Lupien and Oldham's analysis of student research at the University of Guelph consider the message they convey that finding out what is appropriate for your users' needs in your own academic environment is essential to building technology-based services.

References

Armstrong, A. (2012). Marketing the library's instructional services to teaching faculty: Learning from teaching faculty interviews. In L. M. Duke & A. D. Asher (Eds.), *College libraries and student culture: What we now know* (pp. 31–48). Chicago: American Library Association.

ARL. (2012). LibQUAL+ Services: Services and fees. Retrieved from *http://www.libqual.org/about/about_lq/fee_schedule#benefits*

Asher, A. D., & Duke, L. M. (2012). Conclusions and future research. In L. M. Duke & A. D. Asher (Eds.), *College libraries and student culture: What we now know* (pp. 161–167). Chicago: American Library Association.

Asher, A. D., Miller, S., & Green, D. (2012). Ethnographic research in Illinois academic libraries: The ERIAL Project. In L. M. Duke & A. D. Asher (Eds.), *College libraries and student culture: What we now know* (pp. 1–14). Chicago: American Library Association.

Bell, S. (2011, 13 July). Keeping the antennae up: How listening in the library improves UX. [Designing Better Libraries weblog comment]. Retrieved from *http://dbl.lishost.org/blog/2011/07/13/keeping-the-antennae-up-how-listening-in-the-library-improves-ux*

Booth, C. (2009). *Informing innovation: Tracking student interest in emerging library technologies at Ohio University*. Chicago: Association of College & Research Libraries.

Cataldo, T., Freund, L., Ochoa, M., & Salcedo, M. (2007). The info commons concept: Assessing user needs. *Public Services Quarterly, 2*(4), 23–46.

Crump, M. J. (2006). Matrix teams: Advancing transitions. In R. Bazirjian & R. Mugridge (Eds.), *Teams in library technical services* (pp. 207–216). Lanham, MD: Scarecrow Press.

Dahlstrom, E., de Boor, T., Grunwald, P., & Vockley, M., with a foreward by Diana Oblinger. (2011). *The ECAR national study of undergraduate students and information technology, 2011* [research report]. Boulder, CO: EDUCAUSE Center for Applied Research. Retrieved from *http://net.educause.edu/ir/library/pdf/ERS1103/ERS1103W.pdf*

Delacore, H.D., Mullooly, J., & Scroggins, M. (2009). *The library study at Fresno State*. Fresno, CA: Institute of Public Anthropology, California State University, Fresno. Retrieved from *http://www.fresnostate.edu/socialsciences/anthropology/documents/ipa/TheLibraryStudy%28DelcoreMulloolyScroggins%29.pdf*

Duke, L. M. (2012). Transformative changes in thinking, service and programs. In L. M. Duke & A. D. Asher (Eds.), *College libraries and student culture: What we now know* (pp. 143–160). Chicago: American Library Association.

Forrest, C. (2009). Academic libraries as learning spaces: Library effectiveness and user experience. *Georgia Library Quarterly, 46*(3), 7–10.

Foster, N. F. (2007). The mommy model of service. In N. F. Foster & S. Gibbons (Eds.), *Studying students: The undergraduate research project at the University of Rochester* (pp. 72–78). Chicago: Association of College and Research Libraries.

Foster, N. F., & Gibbons, S. (2007). Introduction to the undergraduate research project. In N. F. Foster & S. Gibbons (Eds.), *Studying students: The undergraduate research project at the University of Rochester* (pp. v–vii). Chicago: Association of College and Research Libraries.

Fox, R. & Doshi, A. (2011). *Library user experience*. ARL SPEC Kit 322. Washington, DC: Association of Research Libraries.

Gibbons, S., & Foster, N. F. (2007). Conclusion: Creating student-centered academic libraries. In N. F. Foster & S. Gibbons (Eds.), *Studying students: The undergraduate research project at the University of Rochester* (pp. 79–83). Chicago: Association of College and Research Libraries.

Johnson, L., Smith, R., Willis, H., Levine, A., & Haywood, K. (2011). *The 2011 Horizon Report*. Austin, TX: The New Media Consortium.

Long, M. P., & Schonfeld, R. C. (2010). *Ithaka S+R library survey 2010: Key insights from US academic library directors*. New York: ITHAKA.

Lowry, C. B. (2011). We don't know what the future will be, only that there will be one: The ARL 2030 scenarios project, In S. Hiller, K. Justh, M. Kyrillidou, & J. Self (Eds.), *Proceedings of the 2010 Library Assessment Conference: Building effective, sustainable, practical assessment* (pp. 261–266). Washington, DC: Association of Research Libraries.

McRae, H. (2010). *What works: Success in stressful times*. London: Harper Press.

Oakleaf, M. (2011). Are they learning? Are we? Learning outcomes and the academic library. *The Library Quarterly, 81*(1), 61–82. Retrieved from *http://www.jstor.org/stable/10.1086/657444*

Schmidt, A. (2010). New column launch: The user experience. *Library Journal, 135*(1), 28–29.

Schmidt, A. (2010). The user experience: Learn by asking. *Library Journal, 135*(4), 24.

Schmidt, A. (2011). The user experience: Ready for a UX librarian? *Library Journal, 136*(18), 24.

Schonfeld, R. C., & Housewright, R. (2010). *Faculty survey 2009: Insights for libraries, publishers, and societies*. New York: ITHAKA.

Stephens, M. (2008). Taming technolust: 10 steps for planning in a 2.0 world. *Reference and User Services Quarterly, 47*(4), 314–317.

Thompson, B., Kyrillidou, M., & Cook, C. (2012). *LibQUAL+ Lite*. Washington, DC: Association of Research Libraries. Retrieved from *http://www.libqual.org/about/about_lq/LQ-lite*

Waller, C. A., & Hipps, K. (2002). Using LibQual+ and developing a culture of assessment in libraries. *ARL: A Bimonthly Report of Research Library Issues and Actions from ARL, CNI, and SPARC, 221*, 10–11.

Washburn, A., & Bibb, S. C. (2011). Students studying students: An assessment of using undergraduate student researchers in an ethnographic study of library use. *Library and Information Research, 35*(109), 55–66.

Additional resources

Asher, A., & Miller, S. (2011). *So you want to do anthropology in your library? Or a practical guide to ethnographic research in academic libraries*. Retrieved from *http://www.erialproject.org/publications/toolkit/*

Association of College and Research Libraries. (2010). *Value of academic libraries: A comprehensive research review and report*. Researched by Megan Oakleaf. Chicago: Association of College and Research Libraries.

Cook, C., Heath, F., Thompson, B., & Thompson, R. (2002). The search for new measures: The ARL LibQual+ Project – a preliminary report, portal. *Libraries and the Academy, 1*(1), 103–112.

Duke, L. M., & Asher, A. D. (2012). *College libraries and student culture: What we now know*. Chicago: American Library Association.

Foster, N. F., & Gibbons, S. L. (2007). *Studying students: The undergraduate research project at the University of Rochester*. Chicago: Association of College and Research Libraries.

Staley, D. J., & Malenfant, K. J. (2010). *Futures thinking for academic librarians: Higher education in 2025*. Chicago: Association of College & Research Libraries, American Library Association. Retrieved from *http://www.ala.org/acrl/sites/ala.org.acrl/files/content/issues/value/futures2025.pdf*

5

Millennials and technology: putting suppositions to the test in an academic library

Pascal Lupien and Randy Oldham

Abstract: The topic of Millennial students and their use of technology has become extremely popular in the library and higher education literature. Many libraries have responded by exploring and adopting new technologies to meet the perceived needs and expectations of this important user group, but too often librarians make assumptions that may lead them to create new services that do not really respond to what patrons want or need. The results of this research challenge some of the assumptions made by librarians about Millennials and technology, and should help to guide and inform libraries as they establish priorities in developing emerging services.

Key words: academic libraries, emerging services, Millennials, user expectations, user surveys.

"While it is essential to understand and keep up with new technologies and adapt services accordingly, it is equally important to set priorities and make decisions in a context that is informed by knowledge of local users and their needs."

– P. Lupien & R. Oldham, this volume, p. 103

Introduction

Much has been written in the library and higher education literature about the Millennial generation and their expectations, interests, and use of technology. Generally considered to include individuals born between the early 1980s and the mid-1990s, the Millennial generation (also known in the literature as the NetGen, Generation Next and Generation Y) is said to be the second largest in North American history (Abram & Luther, 2004). Many researchers and practitioners feel that the significant demographic shift caused by the entry of the Millennials into the workforce and the retirement of the Baby Boomers is the most important trend affecting libraries over the next ten years. Clearly, Millennials will have a significant impact on future user expectations. Researchers in the field of education are writing about how factors such as technology have a significant impact on how Millennials learn and this too will affect the information literacy role of librarians.

Much of what has been written focuses on characteristics of the Millennials that supposedly distinguish them from previous generations, and there are a number of common themes that emerge. A frequent assertion is that Millennials are digital natives rather than digital immigrants and are therefore more comfortable and experienced with technology than previous generations (Palfrey & Gasser, 2008; Prensky, 2001; Shah & Abraham, 2009; Zur & Zur, 2009, 2011). They are attracted to technologies that allow for social interaction yet do not think in terms of "technology" while using these services as they see them as an extension of everyday life (Oblinger, 2005). The strong connection between Millennials and technology is also prevalent in the literature on how they learn and conduct research. According to many writers, the way that Millennials approach learning and research tasks will be shaped by their increasingly technology-dependent world, more self-directed and independent, and more focused on visual cues (DiGilio & Lynn-Nelson, 2004; Lippincott, 2005; Weiler, 2004; Windham, 2005). With respect to the higher education experience, they want technology integrated into their courses (Centre for Digital Education, 2004). A recurring trend suggests that they prefer to use the Internet rather than library resources when conducting information research (Griffiths & Brophy, 2005; Holliday & Li, 2004; Luther, 2003). Another common assertion suggests that for most Millennials, authority and knowledge is secondary to simply getting enough "stuff" (Griffiths & Brophy, 2005; Oblinger, 2003).

A critical assessment of the literature, however, is likely to raise a number of reservations. Most of these authors make fairly broad generalizations about Millennials, but these are either not substantiated by any solid research or are beyond what the empirical evidence would allow us to conclude. Commonly cited works describe Millennials as "special, sheltered, confident, team-oriented, achieving, pressured, conventional, tech-embracing" and as "digital natives in a land of digital immigrants," having "never known a day without a computer" (Howe & Strauss, 2000) or portray them as self-oriented to the point of being narcissistic, attitudes that are further encouraged by the use of social media (Twenge, 2006). For the most part, these generalizations do not take into account possible differences related to gender, ethnicity, or socioeconomic status. The assumptions produced by this literature may lead to a bandwagon effect that encourages libraries to adopt the latest "in thing" and to invest human and financial resources in the creation of new services that do not truly respond to user needs. A deeper understanding of our younger users' preferences and use of technology could help us to avoid this and to focus our efforts on using technology in ways that will actually meet their needs. In other words, we should not just adopt technology for the sake of using technology, but rather build tools and services that match our users' interests, needs, and capabilities. The ability to do so requires librarians to develop a better understanding of their own users by engaging in local, targeted research.

Our research

The University of Guelph is located in the city of Guelph in Ontario, Canada, about one hour west of Toronto. The University of Guelph is a medium-sized research-intensive, learner-centred university. There is a single campus Library and Learning Commons at the University of Guelph. The University of Guelph Library engaged in a local research project intended to explore our users' expectations and use of technology. The results of these user consultations challenge many of the assumptions commonly found in the literature. The research team's mandate was to produce research to help establish priorities and to guide and inform other groups working on the development of emerging services in the library and across campus. The goal was to develop a better understanding of our users in order to be able to make better decisions about how to serve them. In 2007, a survey consisting of 59 short-answer and multiple-choice questions was distributed to all students at the University of Guelph via mass email. Focus groups were held after the survey results were examined. These were intended to flesh out what we learned from the survey by asking questions that did not lend themselves well to the survey format, or that we wanted to explore further by talking to students. The focus groups were conducted by an external facilitator and transcripts of the focus groups were analyzed for recurring themes. In 2010, the research team updated and re-administered the questions in the original 2007 survey in order to track trends. The updated survey (see the appendix to this chapter) contained 53 short-answer and multiple-choice questions.

In 2007, there were 19 316 students enrolled at the University of Guelph and 2706 students responded to the initial survey, a 14 percent response rate. Thirty percent of our respondents in 2007 were male, and 70 percent of respondents were female. In 2010 enrolment at the University of Guelph had risen to 20 991 and the survey garnered 1808 respondents, a 9 percent response rate. Seventy-one percent of respondents in 2010 were female and 29 percent of respondents were male. The remainder of this chapter presents selected results and a discussion of the possible implications this type of user-centred study may have for service development in academic libraries.

Hardware ownership and usage

The literature describes Millennials as being immersed in a world of technology and gadgets. They expect to be able to gather and share information using multiple devices. Their information needs are contextual and contingent on whatever device they happen to be using. They expect their technology and services to be mobile (Johnson, Smith, Willis, Levine, & Haywood, 2011). Recent EDUCAUSE Center for Applied Research (ECAR) surveys show an increase of hardware ownership among Millennials, but the ECAR surveys fail to examine *how* Millennials are using this technology: Millennials may own smartphones, but they could be using them only for phone calls (Smith, Caruso, & Educause, 2010). Our research asked respondents not only *what* hardware they owned, but also *how they used it,* because mere ownership does not indicate the amount and depth of device usage. We have seen that much of the literature on Millennials, based on the "digital natives" idea, assumes a certain comfort level with technology. However, being comfortable or even experienced does not necessarily make students more technologically skilled or literate, or able to use technology efficiently and effectively as a tool for learning, writing, and research.

Respondents were asked what type(s) of computer(s) they owned (Table 5.1). Respondents were able to select multiple options to allow them to indicate if they owned more than one type of computer. In 2007, 66 percent of respondents owned laptops, 51 percent owned desktops, and 1 percent owned tablets. In 2010, 90 percent of respondents owned laptops, 22 percent owned desktops, and 1 percent owned tablets (Appendix, Q. 10). In 2010, respondents were asked to identify what operating systems were on the computer(s) they owned. Respondents were permitted to select multiple operating systems to allow them to indicate if they had multiple operating systems installed on a single computer, and to permit those with multiple computers to identify the operating system(s) installed on each of their computers. Ninety-two percent of respondents indicated that their computer(s) had some version of Microsoft Windows installed, 21 percent indicated they had MAC OS installed and 4 percent had a version of Linux installed (Appendix, Q. 11).

In 2010, respondents who indicated that they owned a laptop or tablet were asked how often they brought their laptop/tablet to campus, to class and to the library (Table 5.2). Thirty-five percent of respondents with laptops/tablets indicated that they brought their laptops/tablets to campus daily. Twenty-two percent brought their laptops/tablets to campus weekly (Appendix, Q. 12).

Table 5.1   Computer ownership

	2007	2010	Delta
Laptop	66%	90%	+24%
Desktop	51%	22%	−29%
Tablet	1%	1%	0%

Table 5.2   Frequency of bringing laptop/tablet to campus locations

	To campus	To class	To library
Never	9%	26%	16%
Once a month or less	18%	18%	26%
Several times per month	16%	13%	25%
Several times per week	22%	21%	25%
Daily	35%	22%	8%

The percentage of students who own laptops has increased significantly in the past few years, along with a simultaneous decline in the percentage of desktop owners. This is likely attributable to the decreasing cost and increasing portability of laptop computers. Given that the recent ECAR survey found that desktop ownership appears to be stabilizing, this is perhaps an area that individual libraries should examine, as the trend is likely to vary from one institution to the next (Smith et al., 2010). Being aware of desktop vs. laptop ownership trends among library patrons is obviously important with respect to planning services, but it is also necessary to consider how patrons are using their computers. For example, despite a sharp increase in laptop ownership, this study reveals that only a small minority of patrons actually bring their laptops to the library on a regular basis, despite extensive free wireless access available on campus and in the library. This has important service planning implications. The ownership figures may suggest less of a need for computers in the library because a majority of patrons can bring their own portable computers with them. Yet the fact that they are not doing so should cause librarians to reassess this position. In fact, we have seen that a large percentage of students prefer to use desktop computers in the library. For whatever reason, a majority of students (including many who own a laptop) prefer not to bring them to the library on a regular basis, which suggests the continued need for computers in the library.

In both 2007 and 2010, respondents were asked if they owned a cellphone. In 2007, 69 percent of respondents owned a cellphone and in 2010, 93 percent of respondents owned a cellphone (Appendix, Q. 16). In 2010, respondents who indicated that they owned a cellphone were asked if their cellphone was a smartphone. Twenty-one percent of respondents in 2010 who indicated they owned a cellphone had a smartphone (Appendix, Q. 16). Of these, 62 percent of smartphones were Blackberries, 27 percent were iPhones, and 11 percent were other brands of smartphones (Appendix, Q. 17). Respondents who indicated they owned a cellphone were asked how often they used various features available (Table 5.3). In 2007, 32 percent of respondents browsed the Internet on their cellphones once a month or more frequently, 69 percent took photos, 6 percent viewed videos, and 79 percent sent/received text messages once a month or more frequently. In 2010, 26 percent of respondents browsed the Internet on their cellphone once a month or more frequently, 80 percent took photos, 11 percent viewed videos, and 98 percent sent/received text messages at least once a month or more frequently (Appendix, Q. 18).

Table 5.3	Cellphone feature usage, several times per month or more frequently

	2007	2010	Delta
Browse Internet	32%	26%	−6%
Take photos	69%	80%	+11%
View video	6%	11%	+5%
Text	79%	98%	+19%

While the literature suggests that Millennials expect all services to be accessible through portable devices, this study demonstrates that while the vast majority of our respondents own a cellphone, relatively few own a smartphone. Furthermore, it appears there has been a decrease over the past few years in the number of respondents who browse the Internet using their cellphone. These low figures may seem surprising considering the broad assumptions made in much of the library and education literature. To some extent, the results of this study may be due to the exceptionally high cost of cellphone data plans in Canada in comparison with Europe, and with the United States (where much of the literature on Millennials' use of technology is produced). Perhaps due to cost, respondents do not frequently use features such as web browsing, despite claims made in the literature that they expect all services to be available from mobile devices. Still, these numbers should cause librarians to think more carefully about service development priorities. It makes little sense to invest large amounts of financial and human resources into developing services that can be accessed through mobile devices unless we are quite certain that the majority of our users can both access these services and are interested in doing so. We therefore need to carefully consider how much we should currently invest in making our services available through these mobile devices but should continue to monitor trends, as these could change rapidly and may determine investment priorities in the future.

Online courses

In a report by the Centre for Digital Education (2004), authors comment that Millennials want technology integrated into courses. The fact that Millennials are immersed in technology also suggests that they may prefer courses that are delivered entirely via an online environment to those that are in-class only, or even hybrid courses. There has been a push to suggest that libraries should be investing more time and energy into developing online tutorials to integrate into courses (Centre for Digital Education, 2004; Kelley & Orr, 2003).

Results from our research suggest that the reality may be somewhat more complex. Respondents were asked if they had ever taken an online course at the University of Guelph. In 2007, 63 percent of respondents had taken an online course and, in 2010, that number had dropped to 61 percent (Appendix, Q. 20). Respondents who had taken an online course were asked if they preferred online courses to in-class courses (Appendix, Q. 21). In 2007, 43 percent of respondents did not prefer online courses to in-class, 10 percent preferred online courses to in-class, 23 percent were not sure, and 24 percent did not respond. In 2010, 68 percent of respondents did not prefer online courses to in-class courses, 13 percent did prefer online courses to in-class courses, and 19 percent were not sure (Table 5.4).

Given that there has been a push from some sectors for libraries to transfer the delivery of information literacy instruction to an online environment (through the creation of online tutorials), it is important for libraries to test these claims before moving forward. Contrary to what the literature suggests, respondents in this study do not prefer online courses to in-person contact. Furthermore, when the data is broken down by age, we see no significant difference among the younger students (those under 20 years of age). Students were also asked to specify what they liked or disliked about online courses (Appendix, Q. 22). Many of the "likes" were related to flexibility, convenience, and the ability to work at one's own pace. The "dislikes" were more relevant to the actual effect on student learning, including the lack of interaction with faculty and classmates, impersonal and isolating nature of online courses, having to read large amounts of information from a screen,

Table 5.4 Digital education preference comparison

	2007	2010	Delta
Do not prefer to in-class	43%	68%	+25%
Prefer to in-class	10%	13%	+3%
Not sure	23%	19%	−4%
N/A	24%	0%	−24%

decreased motivation and distraction difficulties, and the heightened likelihood of putting online courses "on the back burner" and not taking them as seriously. Students in the focus groups reinforced this concern with online course delivery. The main problem identified was a lack of accountability in an online environment. Most participants said that if they were going to be asked to work on group projects, they preferred in-person contact, as they could more easily ensure that each group member was accountable.

Respondents were asked if they had taken hybrid courses and they were asked about their preference for hybrid courses (Appendix, Q. 23). A hybrid course is an in-class course that includes an online component. In 2007, 91 percent of respondents had taken a hybrid course, 8 percent had not, and 1 percent did not respond. In 2010, 93 percent of respondents had taken a hybrid course, 6 percent had not, and 1 percent did not respond. Respondents were also asked to indicate their preference for hybrid courses to those courses that were only delivered in-class (Appendix, Q. 24). In 2007, 74 percent of respondents preferred hybrid courses to courses that were only in-class, 8 percent did not prefer hybrid courses to in-class only courses, 12 percent were not sure, and 6 percent did not respond. In 2010, 63 percent preferred hybrid courses to in-class only courses, 20 percent did not prefer hybrid courses (Table 5.5).

Many courses now bridge the divide between online courses and traditional in-class courses by adding an online component to a traditional course through software such as Blackboard or Desire to Learn (D2L). A majority of respondents do claim to prefer courses that offer an online component to a course that does not. In other words, while students prefer in-person learning to strictly online content delivery, they do like to be able to access the course online to download the instructor's notes, post questions about the course, and download readings, and so on. Still, the prevalence of comments about the need for interaction with instructors and classmates suggests that students still

Table 5.5 Hybrid course preference

	2007	2010	Delta
Do not prefer to in-class	8%	20%	+12%
Prefer to in-class	74%	63%	−11%
Not sure	12%	17%	−5%
N/A	6%	0%	−6%

prefer to learn through human contact rather than strictly through technology. All of this suggests that libraries should be wary of calls to go too far in moving instructional content to an online environment, but should rather seek to maintain a balance between online and in-person library educational experiences for students. They may also wish to explore the use of online environments as a follow-up to workshops and in-class sessions.

Social software and gaming

A recurring trend in the literature is the extent to which the Millennials are attracted to technologies that allow for social interaction. The literature indicates that this generation is inclined to be emotionally open and uninhibited on the Internet, that they value freedom of information and choice, and that they are innovative and technology savvy (Leung, 2003; Tappscott, 1998). Technologies that can act as a virtual surrogate for person-to-person contact, allowing for bonds to be created over the web, are very attractive to this generation. Leung (2003) associates these attributes to Internet usage, claiming that those who display these characteristics are more likely to be heavy Internet users. While there is certainly much to be learned from these types of studies, they also demonstrate the weaknesses prevalent in much of the education and information science literature on Millennials. As Leung herself acknowledges, her own study was conducted with a relatively limited geographically concentrated sample and may not be generalizable. Furthermore, Leung's study, like many others that discuss attributes of the Millennials, does not account for differences such as socioeconomic status (in fact, her study excluded anyone who did not have access to the Internet at home). It is therefore necessary to ask whether the conclusions that appear in the literature related to use of social software and gaming are applicable to this generation as a whole, or only a particular segment of that population. Furthermore, these studies generally look at Millennials' use of technology for social purposes and do not attempt to interpret what this may mean for those involved in the academic world.

Many libraries have interpreted these general findings to mean that they should begin to offer services through existing social software, such as Facebook. But can we assume that the extensive use of these tools for social purposes will extend into the academic realm as well? Respondents were asked how often they use social software (such as Facebook,

MySpace, and Google Groups) for academic projects (Appendix, Q. 32). In 2007, 50 percent of respondents had never used social software for academic work, 35 percent had used social software on a few academic projects, 11 percent had on most projects, 3 percent had used social software on every academic project, and 1 percent did not respond. In 2010, 37 percent of respondents had never used social software for academic work, 42 percent had used it on few academic projects, 16 percent on most projects, and 5 percent had used social software on every academic project (Table 5.6). While the trend is that more respondents are using social software for academic purposes, the numbers remain low.

The survey and focus group results suggest that respondents are reluctant to mix personal and academic computing. They enjoy the social aspect of sites such as Facebook and want to keep these separate from their academic lives. As a result, the uptake on online social networks (OSNs) for academic use has been slow, but may increase as younger students more accustomed to these sites move through the education system.

The survey also asked respondents an open-ended question about how OSNs could be useful for academic work (Appendix, Q. 33). A majority of respondents felt that OSNs could be useful for communicating and collaborating with group members. Google Docs was mentioned by a number of respondents as a tool that many are already using for group work. Many respondents felt that OSNs could also be used to connect with other students in their courses and program to exchange information about courses, professors, jobs, and to buy/sell textbooks. The focus group participants confirmed the trends that emerged from the survey. Participants preferred to use social software for social purposes, as there was a clear lack of interest in using it for academic purposes. Most participants said that tools such as Facebook simply would not be as "fun" if they had to use them for academic work. This was the consensus among all participants that used OSNs, including the younger ones.

Table 5.6   **Frequency of social software use on academic projects**

	2007	2010	DELTA
Never	50%	37%	−13%
On few projects	35%	42%	+7%
On most projects	11%	16%	+5%
On every project	3%	5%	+2%
N/A	1%	0%	−1%

These results suggest that the investment of resources to develop services using OSNs may be premature at this point, although libraries should continue to monitor trends with their own users. It appears as though students will only use library tools and services developed using OSNs if they perceive that these are useful and address a need that they have. They will not use them simply for the sake of using technology, which calls into question initiatives such as creating a library Facebook site that has no apparent benefit other than promoting library services. The priority for the investment of resources should involve promoting and providing training and support for existing technologies that may be useful for academic purposes, such as Google Docs, which students are already using for academic tasks.

We are also frequently told that Millennials are into gaming and virtual worlds (Sweeney, 2005; Turkle, 1998). According to this literature, these behaviours can be converted into skills for searching and gaining knowledge. This sometimes translates into suggestions that libraries should make their tutorials more game-like or that vendors should build gaming characteristics into their software (see, for example, Buback, 2007; Levine, 2006). Once again, however, it is not clear that the conclusions made in the literature are generalizable to all members of the Millennial generation. According to our local study, assuming that all people in this population group are into gaming and that services should be designed accordingly may not yield the intended results.

In 2010, respondents were asked how often they play games online (Appendix, Q. 34). Seventy-eight percent of respondents had never played online games, 9 percent had once a month or less, 6 percent several times a month, 5 percent several times a week, and 2 percent several times a day. When reviewing the results by gender, of the 78 percent of respondents who had never played online games, 23 percent of those were male and 77 percent were female. Of the 2 percent who played online games several times a day, 62 percent were male and 38 percent were female (Table 5.7).

This low number may be attributable to the fact that the University of Guelph has a very high percentage of female students. Much of the library and education literature refers to Millennials as a group and does not address potential gender differences. The gender-based literature, however, suggests that females are far less likely to play online games than their male counterparts (Ogletree & Drake, 2007; Winn & Heeter, 2009). The results of our own research demonstrate that males were three times more likely than females to play online games on a regular

Table 5.7 Frequency of online gaming and gender

	Percentage of respondents	Percent male	Percent Female
Never	78%	23%	77%
Less than once a month	9%	–	–
Several times a month	6%	43%	43%
Several times a week	5%	44%	44%
Several times a day	2%	62%	38%

basis. Given these findings, librarians must think carefully about investing resources in building gaming features into online library services. The gender gap with respect to gaming suggests a careful approach to this type of initiative so as not to leave some users behind by adopting certain technologies.

Student research habits

A number of studies have looked more specifically at how Millennials conduct information research. A recurring trend suggests that they prefer to use the Internet rather than library resources (Abram & Luther, 2003; Griffiths & Brophy, 2005; Holliday & Li, 2004). One important study finds that Internet search engines dominate students' information-seeking strategy. Only 10 percent of students begin with the library catalogue while the vast majority prefer to start with an Internet search engine, primarily Google (Griffiths & Brophy, 2005). The vast majority of students (73 percent according to a study of 27 colleges and universities in the United States) claim to use the Internet more than the library. In the above-mentioned study, only 9 percent of students say they use the library more than the Internet (Jones & Madden, 2002). There are a number of explanations for this. Some have found that using the web is simply easier and that the students are far better at surfing the web than the library catalogue, which students often have trouble locating in the first place (Hughes, 2005).

Our research sought to test these generalizations by asking respondents about how often they use various tools to find resources for research assignments (Appendix, Q. 38). In 2007, 73 percent of respondents indicated that they used Google to find resources for their research assignments; 66 percent of respondents used journal indexes; 64 percent had used the online public access catalogue; 41 percent had used Google Scholar and 11 percent had used the research help desk. In 2010, 71 percent of respondents had used Google to find resources for their research assignments; 75 percent had used journal indexes; 60 percent had used the Online Public Access Catalogue (OPAC); 60 percent had used Google Scholar; 7 percent had used the research help desk and 37 percent had used Wikipedia (Table 5.8).

This study shows that our students do use the library in large numbers, and that they appear to understand that they must use a variety of resources, including academic sources, to conduct research. Respondents were asked in 2007 and 2010 to note the first place they go to find information and sources for research assignments (Appendix, Q. 37). They were given the opportunity to provide open-ended answers to avoid leading them to mention library-related resources. The vast majority of respondents did in fact indicate that they begin their research using library-related resources. If all the library-related answers are combined (library website, journal indexes, OPAC, etc.) they would account for more than 80 percent of the answers provided for this open-ended question. This suggests that the vast majority of our respondents are aware of the importance of using Library resources for their research and turn to the library first when beginning a research project. The focus groups confirmed that most students generally use a combination of Library databases, Google Scholar, and Google to find sources for their

Table 5.8 Frequency of tool use to find resources for research assignments

	2007	2010	Delta
Google	73%	71%	−2%
Journal indexes	66%	75%	+9%
OPAC	64%	60%	−4%
Google Scholar	41%	60%	+19%
Research help desk	11%	7%	−4%
Wikipedia	−	37%	−

assignments. They tend to start off doing a broad search and then try to refine the results. However, while students seem to realize that the library has the "best" information for research projects, they also find it to be the most complicated option. The library website, journal indexes, and the OPAC are considered to be frustrating and confusing by users. Students know they must rely on "library stuff," but they find it hard to get to sources and complain that they have to jump through too many hoops.

It is not necessarily the case that students avoid using library resources. They likely do use library resources when they are instructed to and believe that doing so is necessary to complete an assignment, but find the process complicated and frustrating. This suggests that rather than devoting resources to the development of new services, libraries may be serving their users better by enhancing and improving existing search tools. Student feedback suggests two priorities: making the library website more user-friendly and making the search process easier, with more intuitive, less complicated interfaces.

Conclusion

Many of the results discussed above reflect general tendencies, while others appear to challenge many of the common assumptions made in the literature. This suggests that it is useful to share results such as those in this study, as they have several implications that may apply to similar libraries. However, the results also suggest a need for librarians to engage in local user experience work, through surveys, focus groups, and other methods. This will help to ensure that libraries are both aware of general trends and also responsive to the particular needs of their user group.

Libraries are at the cutting edge of many new technologies on university campuses. Caution must be exercised that the development of new services does not become one dimensional, driven only by what is reportedly new and exciting, or the pressure to keep up with what other institutions are doing. Much of the library literature too quickly accepts assertions made about technology and students' use of technology without appropriate critical analysis. While it is essential to understand and keep up with new technologies and adapt services accordingly, it is equally important to set priorities and make decisions in a context that is informed by knowledge of local users and their needs. As the "academic town square" in a learner-centred institution, libraries should engage in evidence-based service planning based on their own students' behaviours, trends, and practices. To this end, libraries should undertake regular studies to identify their students' research and technology needs and to recommend solutions to meet these needs.

References

Abram, S., & Luther, J. (2004). Born with the Chip: The next generation will profoundly impact both library service and the culture within the profession. *Library Journal, 129*(8), 34.

Bubak, S. (2007, 22 August). Libraries: Not just for books anymore. *McMaster Daily News.* Retrieved from *http://dailynews.mcmaster.ca/story.cfm?id=4868*

Centre for Digital Education. (2004). Digital community colleges and the coming of the "millenials": Report of major findings from the Center for Digital Education's 2004 Digital Community Colleges Survey (Higher Ed Special Report). *Technological Horizons In Education Journal, 32*(3), 14–16.

DiGilio, J. J., & Lynn-Nelson, G. (2004). The millennial invasion: Are you ready? *Information Outlook, 8*(11), 15–20.

Griffiths, J. R., & Brophy, P. (2005). Student searching behaviour and the web: Use of academic resources and Google. *Library Trends, 53*(4), 539–555.

Holliday, W., & Li, Q. (2004). Understanding the millennials: Updating our knowledge about students. *Reference Services Review, 32*(4), 356–366.

Howe, N., & Strauss, W. (2000). *Millennials rising.* New York: Vintage Books.

Hughes, H. (2005). Actions and reactions: Exploring international students' use of online information resources. *Australian Academic & Research Libraries, 36*(4), 169–180.

Johnson, L., Smith, R., Willis, H., Levine, A., & Haywood, K. (2011). *The 2011 Horizon Report.* Austin, TX: The New Media Consortium.

Jones, S., & Madden, M. (2002). The Internet goes to college. *Pew Internet and American Life Project.* Retrieved from *http://www.pewinternet.org/About-Us/Our-Research/Use-Policy.aspx*

Kelley, K., & Orr, G. (2003). Trends in distant student use of electronic resources: A survey. *College & Research Libraries, 64*(3), 176–191.

Leung, L. (2003). Impacts of Net-generation attributes, seductive properties of the Internet, and gratifications-obtained on Internet use. *Telematics and Informatics, 20*(2), 107–129.

Levine, J. (2006). Gaming and libraries: Intersection of services. *Library Technology Reports, 42*(5), 5–80.

Lippincott, J. K. (2005). Net generation students and libraries. *EDUCAUSE Review, 40*(2), 56–66.

Luther, J. (2003). Trumping Google? Metasearching's promise. *Library Journal, 128*(16): 36–9.

Nishant, S., & Sunil, A. (2009). *Digital natives with a cause?* Retrieved from *http://cis-india.org/digital-natives/blog/uploads/dnrep1*

Oblinger, D. (2003). Boomers, Gen-Xers and Millennials: Understanding the new students. *EDUCAUSE Review, 38*(4), 37–47.

Oblinger, D. (2005). Asking the right question. *EDUCAUSE Review, 40*(2), 76.

Ogletree, S., & Drake, R. (2007). College students' video game participation and perceptions: Gender differences and implications. Sex *Roles, 37*(7–8): 537–542.

Palfrey, J., & Gasser, U. (2008). *Born digital: Understanding the first generation of digital natives*. New York: Basic Books.

Prensky, M. (2001). Digital natives, digital immigrants. *On the Horizon, 9*(5), 1–6.

Shah, N., & Abraham S. (2009). *Digital natives with a cause?* Raamweg, The Netherlands: Humanist Institute for Cooperation with Developing Countries.

Smith, S. D., Caruso, J. B., & EDUCAUSE Center for Applied Research. (2010). *The ECAR study of undergraduate students and information technology, 2010.* Boulder, CO: Educause Center for Applied Research.

Sweeney, R. T. (2005). Reinventing library buildings and services for the millennial generation. *Library Leadership and Management, 19*(4), 165–175.

Tappscott, D. (1998). *Growing up digital: The rise of the net generation.* New York: McGraw-Hill.

Turkle, S. (1998). Constructions and reconstructions of the self in virtual reality: Playing in the MUDs. In S. Kiesler (Ed.), *Culture of the Internet* (pp. 143–155). Mahwah, NJ: Lawrence Erlbaum.

Twenge, J. (2006). *Generation me: Why today's young Americans are more confident, assertive, entitled – and more miserable than ever before.* New York: Free Press.

Weiler, A. (2004). Information-seeking behaviour in Generation Y students: Motivation, critical thinking, and learning theory. *Journal of Academic Librarianship, 31*(1), 46–53.

Windham, C. (2005). Father Google and mother IM: Confessions of a NetGen learner. *Educause Review, 40*(5), 42–59.

Winn, J., & Heeter C. (2009). Gaming, gender, and time: Who makes time to play? *Sex Roles, 61,* 1–13.

Zur, O., & Zur, A. (2009). *Psychology of the Web & Internet addiction.* Retrieved from

http://www.zurinstitute.com/internetaddiction.html

Zur, O., & Zur, A. (2011). *On digital immigrants & digital natives: How the digital divide affects families, educational institutions, and the workplace.* Retrieved from

http://www.zurinstitute.com/digital_divide.html

Appendix

There are 53 questions in this survey

Student Information

Tell us a bit about you

1 Please indicate your sex *

Please choose **only one** of the following:

- ○ Male
- ○ Female
- ○ Other

2 Please enter your age

Please write your answer here:

3 Please indicate your academic status:

Please choose **only one** of the following:

- ○ Undergraduate Student
- ○ Masters Student
- ○ Doctorate (PhD)

4 Are you a full-time or part-time student?

Please choose **only one** of the following:

- ○ Full-time
- ○ Part-time

5 How many semesters have you completed at the University of Guelph?

Please choose **only one** of the following:

- ○ One Semester
- ○ Two Semesters
- ○ Three Semesters
- ○ Four Semesters
- ○ Five Semesters

- O Six Semesters
- O Seven Semesters
- O Eight Semesters
- O More than eight semesters

There are 3 semesters total per academic year (fall, winter and summer semesters). Most students attend 2 semesters per year, the fall semester and the winter semester.

6. Do you live on campus in a University of Guelph residence building?

Please choose **only one** of the following:

- O Yes
- O No

On campus residences include: MacDonald, Lennox/Addington, Watson, Lambton, Mills, Johnston, East, South.

7 What degree program are you currently registered in?

Please choose **only one** of the following:

- O BA
- O BAS
- O BASc
- O BComm
- O BComp
- O BSAG
- O BSc
- O BSEn
- O BSES
- O MA
- O MAN
- O MBA
- O MEng
- O MLA
- O MSc
- O PhD

- ○DVM
- ○DVSc
- ○Other

8 What major are you currently registered in?

Please write your answer here:

Example: Sociology, Biology, Agricultural Economics, etc.

Hardware

9 Do you have a computer for your own personal use?

Please choose **only one** of the following:

- ○Yes
- ○No

10 Please indicate below which type(s) of computers you have:

Only answer this question if the following conditions are met:
°Answer was 'Yes' at question '9' (Do you have a computer for your own personal use?)

Please choose **all that apply**:

- ☐Desktop
- ☐Laptop (A portable computer/notebook/netbook)
- ☐Tablet (a special type of laptop with a screen that you can write on and which lacks a physical keyboard

11 What operating system(s) are on the computer(s) that you own and regularly use?

Only answer this question if the following conditions are met:
° Answer was 'Yes' at question '9' (Do you have a computer for your own personal use?)

Please choose **all that apply**:

- ☐Windows 7 (any edition)
- ☐Windows Vista (any edition)
- ☐Windows XP
- ☐Windows 2000

- ☐Windows ME (Millennium Edition)
- ☐Windows 98
- ☐Windows 95
- ☐Mac OS (Apple's Operating System)
- ☐Linux (any version)
- ☐Other:

Check all that apply.

12 You stated that you own a laptop and/or tablet. How frequently do you bring your laptop/tablet to campus?

Only answer this question if the following conditions are met:
° Answer was 'Laptop (A portable computer/notebook/netbook)' or 'Tablet (a special type of laptop with a screen that you can write on and which lacks a physical keyboard' at question '10' (Please indicate below which type(s) of computers you have:) *and* Answer was 'Laptop (A portable computer/notebook/netbook)' or 'Tablet (a special type of laptop with a screen that you can write on and which lacks a physical keyboard' at question '10' (Please indicate below which type(s) of computers you have:)

Please choose **only one** of the following:

- ☐Daily
- ☐Several times a week
- ☐Several times a month
- ☐Once a month or less
- ☐Never

If you live in RESIDENCE, please let us know how often you bring your laptop/tablet to a location on campus that is OUTSIDE of your residence building.

13 Why do you rarely/never bring your laptop/tablet to campus?

Only answer this question if the following conditions are met:
° Answer was 'Laptop (A portable computer/notebook/netbook)' or 'Tablet (a special type of laptop with a screen that you can write on and which lacks a physical keyboard' at question '10' (Please indicate below which type(s) of computers you have:) *and* Answer was 'Laptop (A portable computer/notebook/netbook)' or 'Tablet (a special type of

laptop with a screen that you can write on and which lacks a physical keyboard' at question '10' (Please indicate below which type(s) of computers you have:) *and* Answer was 'Never' at question '12' (You stated that you own a laptop and/or tablet. How frequently do you bring your laptop/tablet to campus?) *and* Answer was 'Never' at question '12' (You stated that you own a laptop and/or tablet. How frequently do you bring your laptop/tablet to campus?)

Please write your answer here:

14 Where do you use your laptop/tablet on campus?

Only answer this question if the following conditions are met: ° Answer was 'Laptop (A portable computer/notebook/netbook)' or 'Tablet (a special type of laptop with a screen that you can write on and which lacks a physical keyboard' at question '10' (Please indicate below which type(s) of computers you have:) *and* Answer was 'Laptop (A portable computer/notebook/netbook)' or 'Tablet (a special type of laptop with a screen that you can write on and which lacks a physical keyboard' at question '10' (Please indicate below which type(s) of computers you have:)

Please choose the appropriate response for each item:

	Daily	Several times a week	Several times a month	Once a month or less	Never
University Centre (UC)	O	O	O	O	O
McLaughlin Library	O	O	O	O	O
In Class	O	O	O	O	O
Science Complex Atrium	O	O	O	O	O
Lab or Seminar room	O	O	O	O	O
Other building/ public space	O	O	O	O	O

15 Is there somewhere on campus that doesn't have wireless access and you wish it did?

Please write your answer here:

16 Do you own a cellphone or smartphone such as a BlackBerry or iPhone?

Please choose **only one** of the following:

- ○I own a cellphone
- ○I own a smartphone (such as a BlackBerry or iPhone)
- ○I don't own either a cellphone or smartphone

A smartphone is a mobile phone offering advanced capabilities beyond a typical mobile phone, often with computer-like functionality. Examples of smartphones include: BlackBerries iPhones Motorola Q Phones Many HTC brand phones Any phone with a "windows start button" in the lower left of the screen

17 Please indicate what model of "SmartPhone" you own and use most regularly:

Only answer this question if the following conditions are met: ° Answer was 'I own a smartphone (such as a BlackBerry or iPhone)' at question '16' (Do you own a cellphone or smartphone such as a BlackBerry or iPhone?)

Please choose **only one** of the following:

- ○BlackBerry
- ○Apple iPhone
- ○Motorola Q
- ○HTC
- ○Other

A **smartphone** is a mobile phone offering advanced capabilities beyond a typical mobile phone, often with computer-like functionality. Examples of smartphones include:

– BlackBerries
– Apple iPhones
– Motorola Q Phones
– Many HTC brand phones
– Any phone with a "windows start button" in the lower left of the screen

18 How often do you use your cellphone to do the following:

Only answer this question if the following conditions are met:
° Answer was 'I own a cellphone' or 'I own a smartphone (such as a BlackBerry or iPhone)' at question '16' (Do you own a cellphone or smartphone such as a BlackBerry or iPhone?) *and* Answer was 'I own a cellphone' or 'I own a smartphone (such as a BlackBerry or iPhone)' at question '16' (Do you own a cellphone or smartphone such as a BlackBerry or iPhone?)

Please choose the appropriate response for each item:

	Several times a day	Several times a week	Several times a month	Once a month or less	Never	My cellphone is not capable of this feature
Browse the internet	O	O	O	O	O	O
Send/receive text messages	O	O	O	O	O	O
Take photos	O	O	O	O	O	O
Download or watch videos/TV	O	O	O	O	O	O
Send and receive email	O	O	O	O	O	O

19 Do you own a PDA? (a PalmPilot, Treo, iPAQ ...)

Please choose **only one** of the following:

- OYes
- ONo
- ONot sure

Distance Ed, Courselink/Desire2Learn and Open Learning/Desire2Learn

The next set of questions deal with distance education at the University of Guelph.

Open Learning, the University of Guelph Distance Education provider, has used Desire2Learn to deliver online courses for over 5 years now.

Teaching Support Services (TSS) has been supplementing traditional in-class courses with online components for more than 5 years. Initially, these online components were delivered via "Blackboard/WebCT". Over the past 2 years, TSS has been transitioning their online learning environment to Desire2Learn.

20 Have you taken a distance education (Open Learning) course at the University of Guelph?

Please choose **only one** of the following:

- O Yes
- O No

Distance Education courses are offered through OPEN LEARNING at the University of Guelph and have the DE designation in WebAdvisor.

21 In general, do you prefer distance education (Open Learning) courses to traditional in-class courses?

Only answer this question if the following conditions are met:
° Answer was 'Yes' at question '20' (Have you taken a distance education (Open Learning) course at the University of Guelph?)

Please choose **only one** of the following:

- O Yes
- O No
- O Not sure

22 What do you like or dislike about distance education (Open Learning) courses at the University of Guelph?

Only answer this question if the following conditions are met:
° Answer was 'Yes' at question '20' (Have you taken a distance education (Open Learning) course at the University of Guelph?)

Please write your answer here:

23 Have you ever taken an <u>in-class</u> course at the University of Guelph that <u>included</u> an online component such as Desire2Learn/Courselink?

Please choose **only one** of the following:

- O Yes
- O No
- O Not sure

"Courses with an online component" would include those in-class courses which include access to Desire2Learn/Courselink, MyEconLab, etc.

24 Do you prefer in-class courses that <u>include</u> an online component over courses that are <u>only</u> in-class?

Only answer this question if the following conditions are met:
° Answer was 'Yes' or 'Not sure' at question '23' (Have you ever taken an in-class course at the University of Guelph that included an online component such as Desire2Learn/Courselink?) *and* Answer was 'Yes' or'Not sure' at question '23' (Have you ever taken an in-class course at the University of Guelph that included an online component such as Desire2Learn/Courselink?)

Please choose **only one** of the following:

- ○ Yes
- ○ No

"Courses with an online component" would include those in-class courses which include access to Desire2Learn/Courselink, MyEconLab, etc.

25 What do you like or not like about courses that include an online component?

Only answer this question if the following conditions are met:
° Answer was 'Yes' or 'Not sure' at question '23' (Have you ever taken an in-class course at the University of Guelph that included an online component such as Desire2Learn/Courselink?) *and* Answer was 'Yes' or 'Not sure' at question '23' (Have you ever taken an in-class course at the University of Guelph that included an online component such as Desire2Learn/Courselink?)

Please write your answer here:

"Courses with an online component" would include those in-class courses which include access to Desire2Learn/Courselink, MyEconLab, etc.

Online Services

The following set of questions deal with how you use online services such as chatting and online social networks (such as Facebook).

26 Do you use an online chat program such as MSN Messenger (Windows Live Messenger), AIM, ICQ, Facebook chat, Google Talk, Gmail chat, etc?

Please choose **only one** of the following:

- ○Yes
- ○No

27 Please select all of the online chat programs that you use regularly:

Only answer this question if the following conditions are met:
° Answer was 'Yes' at question '26' (Do you use an online chat program such as MSN Messenger (Windows Live Messenger), AIM, ICQ, Facebook chat, Google Talk, Gmail chat, etc?)

Please choose **all** that apply:

- ☐MSN Messenger/Windows Live Messenger
- ☐Yahoo Messenger
- ☐Google Talk
- ☐Gmail chat
- ☐AOL Instant Messenger (AIM)
- ☐ICQ
- ☐Facebook Chat
- ☐Skype Chat
- ☐IRC
- ☐Other:

28 How many hours a day are you actively using a chat program?

Only answer this question if the following conditions are met:
° Answer was 'Yes' at question '26' (Do you use an online chat program such as MSN Messenger (Windows Live Messenger), AIM, ICQ, Facebook chat, Google Talk, Gmail chat, etc?)

Please choose **only one** of the following:

- ○Less than 1 hour a day
- ○1–3 hours a day
- ○4–6 hours a day

- O7 or more hours a day
- OOther

29 How often do you use online chat to discuss <u>academic work with friends or classmates</u>?

Only answer this question if the following conditions are met:
° Answer was 'Yes' at question '26' (Do you use an online chat program such as MSN Messenger (Windows Live Messenger), AIM, ICQ, Facebook chat, Google Talk, Gmail chat, etc?)

Please choose **only one** of the following:

- OSeveral times a day
- OSeveral times a week
- OSeveral times a month
- OOnce a month or less
- ONever

30 How often do you use online chat to communicate with <u>group members about group projects</u>?

Only answer this question if the following conditions are met:
° Answer was 'Yes' at question '26' (Do you use an online chat program such as MSN Messenger (Windows Live Messenger), AIM, ICQ, Facebook chat, Google Talk, Gmail chat, etc?)

Please choose **only one** of the following:

- OOn every project
- OOn most projects
- OOn few projects
- ONever

31 How often do you participate in online social communities such as Facebook, MySpace, Windows Live Spaces?

Please choose **only one** of the following:

- OSeveral times a day
- OSeveral times a week
- OSeveral times a month
- OOnce a month or less
- ONever

Participation in online social communities would include chatting, posting messages, posting pictures, and browsing other members profiles for example.

32 How often have you used online social communities for _academic_ work?

Only answer this question if the following conditions are met:
° Answer was NOT 'Never' at question '31' (How often do you participate in online social communities such as Facebook, MySpace, Windows Live Spaces?) *and* Answer was NOT 'Never' at question '31' (How often do you participate in online social communities such as Facebook, MySpace, Windows Live Spaces?)

Please choose **only one** of the following:

- ○On every project
- ○On most projects
- ○On few projects
- ○Never

33 How are you using online social communities in your _academic_ work? Provide us your comments here:

Only answer this question if the following conditions are met:
° Answer was 'Once a month or less' or 'Several times a month' or 'Several times a week' or 'Several times a day' at question '31' (How often do you participate in online social communities such as Facebook, MySpace, Windows Live Spaces?) *and* Answer was 'Once a month or less' or 'Several times a month' or 'Several times a week' or 'Several times a day' at question '31' (How often do you participate in online social communities such as Facebook, MySpace, Windows Live Spaces?) *and* Answer was 'Once a month or less' or 'Several times a month' or 'Several times a week' or 'Several times a day' at question '31' (How often do you participate in online social communities such as Facebook, MySpace, Windows Live Spaces?) *and* Answer was 'Once a month or less' or 'Several times a month' or 'Several times a week' or 'Several times a day' at question '31' (How often do you participate in online social communities such as Facebook, MySpace, Windows Live Spaces?)

Please write your answer here:

34 How frequently do you do the following:

Please choose the appropriate response for each item:

	Several times a day	Several times a week	Several times a month	Once a month or less	Never
Download music	O	O	O	O	O
Download movies & videos	O	O	O	O	O
Post to sites such as YouTube, MySpace, Facebook	O	O	O	O	O
Post to blogs	O	O	O	O	O
Play online games such as World of Warcraft	O	O	O	O	O
Play games online for money (e.g. poker)	O	O	O	O	O
Participate in online virtual worlds such as Second Life	O	O	O	O	O
Shop online	O	O	O	O	O
Visit an online news site	O	O	O	O	O
Online dating	O	O	O	O	O
Visiting sites related to my hobbies and/ or personal interests	O	O	O	O	O

35 List up to three <u>non</u>-University of Guelph websites that you visit most frequently, other than email websites like Gmail, Hotmail...

Please write your answer(s) here:

- 1)

- 2)

- 3)

36 List up to three University of Guelph websites that you visit most frequently, other than Gryphmail, Desire2Learn/Courselink, webadvisor.

Please write your answer(s) here:

- 1)

- 2)

- 3)

37 Where is the first place you go to find information and sources for your research assignments?

Please write your answer here:

38 How frequently do you use the following tools to find resources (such as books and journal articles) for research assignments?

Please choose the appropriate response for each item:

	Always	Frequently	Sometimes	Rarely	Never	Not sure
Primo/Trellis (U of G's Library Catalogue)	O	O	O	O	O	O
Journal indexes/ journal databases (articles link on library webpage)	O	O	O	O	O	O
Online bookstore (e.g. Amazon.com, Chapters.ca)	O	O	O	O	O	O
Google	O	O	O	O	O	O
Google Scholar	O	O	O	O	O	O
Wikipedia	O	O	O	O	O	O
Classmates/ friends	O	O	O	O	O	O

	Always	Frequently	Sometimes	Rarely	Never	Not sure
Course instructor (Professor)	O	O	O	O	O	O
Teaching Assistant (TA)	O	O	O	O	O	O
Library Research Help Desk	O	O	O	O	O	O
Other	O	O	O	O	O	O

39 You chose "other" in the previous question. Please tell us what "other" tool you use to find resources (such as books and journal articles) for research assignments.

Only answer this question if the following conditions are met: ° Answer was 'Sometimes' or 'Always' or 'Frequently' or 'Rarely' at question '38' (How frequently do you use the following tools to find resources (such as books and journal articles) for research assignments? (Other)) *and* Answer was 'Sometimes' or 'Always' or 'Frequently' or 'Rarely' at question '38' (How frequently do you use the following tools to find resources (such as books and journal articles) for research assignments? (Other)) *and* Answer was 'Sometimes' or 'Always' or 'Frequently' or 'Rarely' at question '38' (How frequently do you use the following tools to find resources (such as books and journal articles) for research assignments? (Other)) *and* Answer was 'Sometimes' or 'Always' or 'Frequently' or 'Rarely' at question '38' (How frequently do you use the following tools to find resources (such as books and journal articles) for research assignments? (Other)).

Please write your answer here:

40 Have you ever contributed a review for books, music or movies to a website?

Please choose **only one** of the following:

- O Yes
- O No

For example, have you ever posted a comment about a book you read to an online bookstore such as Amazon.com, or a review about a movie you saw to a movie site such as IMDB.COM?

41 List up to 3 websites that you've found most useful for searching for information for assignments:

Please write your answer(s) here:

- 1)

- 2)

- 3)

42 List up to 3 websites that you've found most useful for other academic work (i.e. writing papers, managing your time, preparing for tests or exams, etc.)

Please write your answer(s) here:

- 1)

- 2)

- 3)

Communicating about research

43 Have you asked any of the following people for help on a research assignment? If so, how have you communicated with them? Please check all that apply:

	In Person	E-Mail	Phone	Course-specifc Online discussion (through desire2learn...)	Chat (MSN, Google chat...)	Never contacted for research help
Course Instructor (Professor)	☐	☐	☐	☐	☐	☐
TA (teaching assistant)	☐	☐	☐	☐	☐	☐
Lab Instructor	☐	☐	☐	☐	☐	☐
Library Staff	☐	☐	☐	☐	☐	☐
Family Member	☐	☐	☐	☐	☐	☐
Learning Commons Peer Helper	☐	☐	☐	☐	☐	☐
Friend or Classmate	☐	☐	☐	☐	☐	☐
RA (residence assistant) or Res life staff	☐	☐	☐	☐	☐	☐
Other	☐	☐	☐	☐	☐	☐

Check all the methods you have used to contact these types of individuals for help on a research assignment.

44 If you choose OTHER in the previous question, who do you consult for research help that was missing in the previous question?

Please write your answer here:

Library Computers

The next set of questions deal with public desktop & laptop computers in the library.

45 How often have you used a public <u>desktop</u> computer in the library at the University of Guelph?

Please choose **only one** of the following:

- OSeveral times a day
- OSeveral times a week
- OSeveral times a month
- OOnce a month or less
- ONever

46 How long do you typically have to wait to use a public <u>desktop</u> computer in the Library?

Only answer this question if the following conditions are met: ° Answer was 'Several times a day' or 'Several times a week' or 'Several times a month' or 'Once a month or less' at question '45' (How often have you used a public desktop computer in the library at the University of Guelph?) *and* Answer was 'Several times a day' or 'Several times a week' or 'Several times a month' or 'Once a month or less' at question '45' (How often have you used a public desktop computer in the library at the University of Guelph?) *and* Answer was 'Several times a day' or 'Several times a week' or 'Several times a month' or 'Once a month or less' at question '45' (How often have you used a public desktop computer in the library at the University of Guelph?) *and* Answer was 'Several times a day' or 'Several times a week' or 'Several times a month' or 'Once a month or less' at question '45' (How often have you used a public desktop computer in the library at the University of Guelph?) *and* Answer was 'Several times a day' or 'Several times a week' or 'Several times a month' or 'Once a month or less' at question '45' (How often have you used a public desktop computer in the library at the University of Guelph?)

Please choose **only one** of the following:

- OI never have to wait
- OLess than 2 minutes
- OAbout 5 minutes
- OBetween 5 and 10 minutes
- OBetween 10 and 15 minutes
- OLonger than 15 minutes

47 How often have you borrowed a <u>laptop</u> from the library?

Please choose **only one** of the following:

- ○ Several times a day
- ○ Several times a week
- ○ Several times a month
- ○ Once a month or less
- ○ Never

48 How often have you tried to borrow a <u>laptop</u> from the library, but found that there weren't any available and had to wait to sign one out?

Only answer this question if the following conditions are met:
° Answer was 'Several times a day' or 'Several times a week' or 'Several times a month' or 'Once a month or less' at question '47' (How often have you borrowed a laptop from the library?) *and* Answer was 'Several times a day' or 'Several times a week' or 'Several times a month' or 'Once a month or less' at question '47' (How often have you borrowed a laptop from the library?) *and* Answer was 'Several times a day' or 'Several times a week' or 'Several times a month' or 'Once a month or less' at question '47' (How often have you borrowed a laptop from the library?) *and* Answer was 'Several times a day' or 'Several times a week' or 'Several times a month' or 'Once a month or less' at question '47' (How often have you borrowed a laptop from the library?)

Please choose **only one** of the following:

- ○ I never have to wait
- ○ I rarely have to wait
- ○ I sometimes have to wait
- ○ I often have to wait
- ○ I almost always have to wait

49 How frequently do you need to request a renewal for a <u>laptop</u> borrowed from the library because you need it for longer than 2 hours?

Only answer this question if the following conditions are met:
° Answer was 'Several times a day' or 'Several times a week' or 'Several times a month' or 'Once a month or less' at question '47' (How often have you borrowed a laptop from the library?) *and* Answer was 'Several

times a day' or 'Several times a week' or 'Several times a month' or 'Once a month or less' at question '47' (How often have you borrowed a laptop from the library?) *and* Answer was 'Several times a day' or 'Several times a week' or 'Several times a month' or 'Once a month or less' at question '47' (How often have you borrowed a laptop from the library?) *and* Answer was 'Several times a day' or 'Several times a week' or 'Several times a month' or 'Once a month or less' at question '47' (How often have you borrowed a laptop from the library?)

Please choose **only one** of the following:

- O Several times a day
- O Several times a week
- O Several times a month
- O Once a month or less
- O Never

50 The ideal <u>laptop</u> loan period would be:

Please choose **only one** of the following:

- O 2 Hours
- O 3 Hours
- O 4 Hours
- O 8 Hours
- O Other

51 When using a Library computer, do you prefer to use a library laptop, or a desktop?

Please choose **only one** of the following:

- O Laptop
- O Desktop
- O Either... I have no preference.

52 Please tell us why you prefer a library laptop or desktop.

Only answer this question if the following conditions are met:
° Answer was 'Laptop' or 'Desktop' at question '51' (When using a Library computer, do you prefer to use a library laptop, or a desktop?)

and Answer was 'Laptop' or 'Desktop' at question '51' (When using a Library computer, do you prefer to use a library laptop, or a desktop?)

Please write your answer here:

General Comments

53 This is the final question... It's an open invitation for you to include any comments on anything technology-related on campus. Wish there were more outlets in classrooms? Do you experience problems with wireless on campus? Wish the computer lab in your department had new computers? Let us know!

Please write your answer here:

6

We asked and they told us: survey × 2

Michele J. Crump and LeiLani S. Freund

Abstract: This chapter provides the methodology used for the Crump/Freund study and survey tool in detail and analyzes the data results. Each of the five partner libraries participating in this unique study is profiled, including general demographic information for the parent academic institution. The authors then provide a summary of the results of the library user and library staff surveys, respectively. The chapter concludes with an analysis of the survey questions that comprise the comparative study results and may or may not support the authors' supposition that a divide exists between the perceptions of library staff and the needs of the users they serve.

Key words: information commons (IC), institutional review board, library staff, library users, perceptions, survey, survey sample, SurveyMonkey™.

"Students still want their librarians in person (especially when accompanied with a donut) and though many will want our help, it is just a fact that many others simply do not (until, of course, they do)."

– C. C. Barratt, P. Acheson, & E. Luken (2010) Reference models in the electronic library: The Miller Center at the University of Georgia, p. 54

Survey methodology

The study and survey tool developed by the authors has as its objective an examination of the perceptions and preferences of the users as well as the library staff in the information commons (IC) environment of academic libraries. For purposes of the survey, we define IC very broadly to encompass the building that contains, in addition to other services, a large commons area as defined in Chapter 2. The authors developed two surveys, one for library users and one for library staff, primarily intended for (but not limited to) humanities and social sciences libraries or main/multidisciplinary libraries that serve a large undergraduate clientele. The surveys measure responses to the same or similar questions asked of IC users and IC staff to ascertain whether a divide or lack of understanding exists between library service providers and their customers. The complete survey results are available at: *http://guides.uflib.ufl.edu/2011userstaffsurvey*.

In order to expand the study beyond the University of Florida (UF), the authors identified, in the course of preliminary research and the literature review, a number of libraries in the United States that have relatively new implementations of information or learning commons. Some are new constructions and others are renovations of existing buildings, but all have in common a large undergraduate population and innovative approaches to serving their clientele. We offered the surveys, approved by the UF Institutional Review Board (IRB), advice as needed for the distribution of the surveys, and complete, compiled data results that may be used internally until such time as the authors' work is published.

Recruiting partners

The authors contacted key IC personnel at each of the libraries we had targeted as potential partners. Only one library responded; however, this library subsequently became part of the study. We advise other researchers that, in a study of this kind, there are a number of issues that make it difficult to find partners within a reasonably short timeframe: (1) the academic calendar makes it difficult for librarians to ascertain the best time to approach the customers to get the largest sample and yet not annoy those who are busy with exams and papers; (2) the bureaucracy of most large academic institutions precludes a quick response from librarians who may wish to join the study but who need several permissions to do so; (3) there must be adequate lead time for partners to go through their IRBs to obtain permission for human study; (4) many libraries are using survey tools, thus survey burnout (for both patrons and staff) and redundancy is a real concern for many librarians and library administrators; and, finally, (5) accommodation of requests from partners for substantial changes to the survey are not necessarily in the best interests of the principal researchers' goals. In short, partnerships are difficult to negotiate and everyone involved needs to be as flexible as possible.

The next approach we used to find additional survey library partners was to identify appropriate online discussion groups to advertise our research. At this point, we decided that the size of the institution was not an issue, but the existence of a new or nearly new IC and a large undergraduate population remained a requirement. Several interested librarians replied to the first and second calls we made to the very active and relevant INFOCOMMONS-L group. From these responses, we were able to form a small group of five institutions, including UF, able to distribute the survey within the fall semester 2011 timeframe. Although this was not the number of partners we originally envisioned, the libraries represent a variety of regions of the country, have dynamic IC facilities of varying configurations, and all the people involved were enthusiastic and able to cut through the red tape to get the survey underway. Should the survey results fail to show significant trends and instead display more questions than answers, the authors have the option to follow up with the established partners or solicit a new set of libraries for further study. The results presented in this book are intended as a starting point for the comparative research the authors feel is needed to stimulate action within the profession.

The UF's IRB approved the authors' research plan and authorized the surveys for distribution during the academic fall semester of 2011. The partner librarians received copies of the proposal, surveys, consent forms, and approved UF IRB form so they could pursue approval through their own boards, as required by their institutions. None of the partners reported any problems with the research approval process. Some partners suggested minor changes to the survey that improved the logic of the questions and others requested the addition of a few questions to get more local, demographic data. One library added an entry at the end that pertained to a local contest to encourage participation. The authors were amenable to local additions to the survey that would make the survey more meaningful and successful for the partners as long as the original content remained intact.

Sample size and distribution

In 2010, Noaman Adhami, a graduate student in the Interior Design program at the UF, conducted as part of his master's thesis requirement an extensive post-occupancy evaluation of the 2006 Library West (humanities and social sciences library) redesign and renovation that included the creation of the IC. We borrowed the Adhami (2011) calculation of a 0.01 percent or 120-person sample size based on approximately 1.2 million annual visitors (gate count) to the Library West facility in 2010. Adhami made his calculation based on the Agresti and Finlay specifications in the 2009 publication, *Statistical Methods for the Social Sciences* (Adhami, 2011, pp. 50–51). The authors asked the partner librarians to follow a similar calculation for their user survey samples and all but one library met or exceeded the specified percentage.

The authors sent the staff survey link to all UF library staff who met our requirements for time spent in the Library West facility. All of these people had some kind of public service contact with the Library West patrons. We obtained a 60 percent response rate from the targeted UF staff. We asked our partner libraries to try to get as close as possible to full compliance from their public service staff. Staff participation varied widely from library to library. Two libraries had fairly large numbers (about 20 percent and 40 percent, respectively) of staff members who agreed to the terms of the survey but subsequently answered very few or no questions. The authors conjectured that in these cases the survey was probably sent to all staff members, many of whom may not have direct contact with the library users and thus decided after reading the questions that they had little to offer.

It had become apparent within recent months at the UF Libraries that user surveys posted only on the library's home page were obtaining very few respondents. The authors were certain from the beginning that a more personal approach would be needed and we strongly urged the librarians in our partner institutions to do the same. In fact, one library at first tried to post the survey only on the library website and received only one response. As many library colleagues have noted, food does wonders for getting participants. The authors chose chocolate and the personal approach of handing out a flyer that read, "This is your library – Tell us what you think!" and included a link plus a QR code for smartphone users that led the participant directly to the survey. Our rate of participation using this method during the daytime hours was quite impressive. On our best afternoon on the two most crowded floors of the library we obtained a participation rate of over 50 percent of the total number of flyers handed out. The authors decided not to stand at the entrance to the library because after one attempt it was clear that people could too easily avoid our eyes and pass on by. Adhami (2011) had more success at the Library West entrance with a group of student helpers who were more aggressive in making contact. The night IC coordinator, noting that the students seemed much more focused and uninterruptible in the evening, quietly distributed flyers after 8 pm in the IC and on the graduate floor by simply placing the flyers on chairs or near the students. As he predicted, the rate of success at night was lower, never exceeding 30 percent. It's noteworthy that the partner library with the largest user sample size distributed the survey via the web but also had an established relationship with student government that they successfully leveraged for distribution to the students.

All UF-administered surveys were electronically formatted and included full consent forms that the participants could digitally "check" or easily back out of the survey. The consent forms included information regarding the collection of data and the removal of all identifying information, including tracking of computer IP addresses. The surveys were developed with the SurveyMonkey™ software and were deliberately kept short, consisting of 19 questions for the staff and 17 questions for the customers, excluding locally added queries. Test runs showed the time needed to complete the surveys averaging between 10 and 15 minutes. The results of the data compilation are reported anonymously in this book as Library A–E at the request of some of the library participants. Open responses from users and staff were coded by categories, several of which were the same or very similar to the categories devised for local use by the University of California, Santa Cruz partners; the authors gratefully acknowledge their contribution to the process.

Assumptions

The authors' research is best served by surveying users who are actually in the library building that includes the IC. The purpose of this study is not to test perceptions of those who do not or rarely use the library and the IC, but rather those who have some knowledge of the services and features of the building. At UF, the staff survey was limited to employees who perform most or all of their assigned job duties in the Library West facility, or participate in a regular Library West service desk assignment. However, UF has one of the larger staff populations of the five libraries and an organization that accommodates a more targeted approach.

Responses of the participants are unbiased and reflect only their own opinions. Although some of the authors' library staff colleagues were aware that we were planning publication of the study, few were aware of the details or specific research goals. Likewise, the users were told only that we wished to get their opinions on Library West services and facilities. The authors can only conjecture whether the personal approach we took to handing out flyers and obtaining willing participants may have biased the survey. We did in fact get a warm response from some students who seemed appreciative of being asked their opinion. We wondered after the fact if taking the time to talk with the students and make a personal appeal for their participation may have biased their attitudes toward the library or library staff as a whole. However, the alternative would have been to get a poor sample population within our time constraints.

The survey is not a scientific survey per se; we do not have sufficient sampling to test or infer statistical significance. Also, the wide differences between the size of the user and staff populations of our partner libraries and the methodologies they used to obtain samples preclude any meaningful statistical comparison. The purpose of the survey is to ascertain preferences and test perceptual differences that may divide the library staff and library users and to learn how similarly such gaps may manifest in other libraries and locales. We have from the beginning felt that such trends and similarities or differences will be easy to spot and perhaps most obvious, as is often the case with such surveys, in the open comments rather than the controlled questions.

Survey participant profiles

E.S. Bird Library, Syracuse University Library (http://library. syr.edu/)

General information about parent institution: Syracuse University is a predominantly residential campus comprised of the following student demographics as of fall 2011 (*http://library.syr.edu/about/ general-info/welcome/vision.php?print*):

- 13 987 full-time undergraduates
- 684 part-time undergraduates
- 3812 full-time graduates
- 1681 part-time graduates

How surveys were distributed: The Syracuse participants, Associate Dean for Undergraduate Education, Head of the Library's Learning Commons, and Research & Assessment Analyst, distributed the survey through adding a link to the survey tool on Facebook, Twitter, and the library website. This technique gathered less than half of the total received. Distributing the survey to students within the library resulted in almost double the amount completed through the online manner.

How the library will share survey results with customers and library staff: The participants mentioned above created a PowerPoint presentation that summarizes the survey results comparing students' responses with the responses of the library staff. They will present their slide program to Bird Library administrators and library staff working in the Learning Commons. Current plans to institute any service changes are under consideration. Feedback from other studies and the UF survey project indicate that Bird needs to install more electrical outlets and designate additional quiet study areas within the library; future library service changes will take this significant student input into consideration when making plans.

IC in renovated or new building: The Learning Commons in Bird Library was the result of the first floor renovation in 2008. A groundbreaking for a new high-density storage library facility took place in October 2011 (*http://eventful.com/Syracuse/events/bird-library-café-and-learning-commons-grand-openi-/E0-001-009265072-0; http://library.syr.edu/blog/news/archives/2011_10.php*).

Library information: Bird Library houses the humanities and social sciences collections and is considered the main library on the Syracuse campus. The newly renovated first floor contains the Learning Commons and Pages, the library café. The Learning Commons serves its patrons from the Circulation Desk for checking out print and other research resources and the User Technology Support desk for checking out technical equipment such as laptops, netbooks, digital recorders, and cameras. Resident Librarians, a new program initiated in 2009, brings new librarians into the Learning Commons to support reference, outreach, orientation, and group instruction, as well as to develop tools and spark innovation (*http://library.syr.edu/about/departments/ learning_commons/index.php*).

McHenry Library and the Science & Engineering Library, University of California, Santa Cruz (UCSC) (http://library. ucsc.edu/)

General information about parent institution: UCSC is a public institution with 42 percent of the students living in university housing. The following student demographics represent the university student body as of fall 2011:

- 15 945 undergraduates
- 1509 graduates

How surveys were distributed: The UCSC participants, Head of Research, Outreach, and Instruction and Planning & Assessment Librarian, worked with their student government and set up tables at the two libraries from which they distributed fliers. They also posted a link to the survey on their library website, put streamers with the link to the survey on all library computers, and distributed fliers within the libraries.

How the library will share survey results with customers and library staff: The participants are still analyzing the data they received from both surveys. They will use the input from that data to inform future physical layout changes. The participants prepared a slide presentation highlighting preliminary findings and have shared it with the library management group and with public service staff. In addition they have discussed their work on the UF project with the UCSC Academic Senate Committee on the Library and Scholarly Communications. UCSC participants created their own instances of the UF surveys so that they could add demographic information questions at the end of the surveys. By gathering information about students and their college affiliation, they will be able to parse responses by college and offer important data to the provosts concerning students' usage of the library.

IC in renovated or new building: McHenry Library was totally renovated from 2008 to 2011 and a new addition to the building was constructed 2005–08 (Santa Cruz Sentinel.com, 18 February 2012: *http://www.santacruzsenteinel.com/ci_19995664*). The IC is located on the main floor along with the Global Village Café.

Library Information: UCSC has two libraries, the newly renovated and expanded McHenry Library, which houses the humanities and social sciences, and fine arts collections and the Science & Engineering Library, which houses the sciences, video and gaming lab, map & GIS, and the East Asian collection. Both libraries have group study rooms with over 20 located in McHenry in addition to several music listening and video viewing rooms; Science & Engineering has eight group study rooms available for their patrons (*http://library.ucsc.edu/services/study-rooms*).

Valley Library, Oregon State University (OSU) (http://osulibrary.oregonstate.edu/)

General information about parent institution: OSU is a Land Grant institution and the following student demographics represent the university student body as of fall 2011:

- 20 621 undergraduates
- 3776 graduates

How surveys were distributed: The Librarian for Innovative User Services discussed participating in the UF library staff survey during a library management meeting. After the meeting an email was distributed to all library faculty and staff that included an explanation of the survey and a link to the instrument. For users, the Learning Commons Coordinator worked with the library Web Developer to add a pop-up window that displayed on the Learning Commons computers so that only patrons within the library using the Learning Commons were invited to participate.

How the library will share survey results with customers and library staff: Valley Library participants plan to share survey results with library users and staff but are still analyzing survey responses. Once the analysis is evaluated they will determine how to present the data to benefit the library and the Learning Commons as well as make decisions about any changes they might want to make to the collaborative library area.

IC in renovated or new building: In November–December 2010, The Valley Library established the Learning Commons on its main floor in an area that used to house reference stacks. Before the remodeling, students participated in surveys online and in print format to vote on furniture types and space usage, and offered input during focus groups. The new area invites collaboration and learning with the addition of seating, tables, white boards, and media viewing technology to make group viewing possible.

Library information: Valley Library's focus is to use innovation and digital collections to engage and support the research endeavors of students and faculty. To that end the purchase of electronic resources has increased significantly in recent years. The library also participates in several consortia to expand access to research resources for its constituents: Orbis/Cascades Alliance, Great Western Library Alliance, Western Waters Digital Library, and Midwestern & Western (*http://osulibrary.oregonstate.edu/ collections/collaborations*).

University of Texas at San Antonio (UTSA), John Peace Library (http://www.utsa.edu/)

General information about parent institution: Established in 1969, UTSA is a public research institution that serves the following (Data from 2010 *UTSA Fact Book*):

- Total student enrollment: 30 258
- Number of undergraduates: 25 794
- Number of graduates: 4464
- Number of commuters: 27 302
- Number of campus residents: 2956

How surveys were distributed: The Head of the First-Year Services with the User Experience Librarian and the Digital User Experience Librarian distributed the surveys to library staff through email, first explaining the purpose of the survey followed by another email providing the link to the instrument. The student survey was made available on a laptop computer at the Information Desk in the IC. Flyers with the URL were also available and many students used the computers in the IC to respond. Some students took the survey fliers and responded to the survey outside the library (these students were part of the Freshmen Seminar class taught by librarians; students received extra credit for participating).

How the library will share survey results with customers and library staff: John Peace Library is planning a renovation and the results of this survey, both staff and user, will be included in the decision making for new services and facility changes. The participants have also shared some preliminary results with management teams from the IC. Comparative results will be presented to a broader library audience during a weekly leadership meeting.

IC in renovated or new building: The IC area is located on the second floor of the John Peace Library in a renovated space. The area offers collaborative, quiet study, a multipurpose room, presentation room, media viewing rooms, as well as the Multimedia

Center and Tutorial Services. The second floor is also home to the Adaptive Technology Computer Lab (*http://lib.utsa.edu/about/about-the-utsa-libraries/*).

Library information: John Peace Library serves its community with an emphasis on "providing access to the best, most current information resources available, placing special emphasis on digital materials in order to designate as much physical space as possible for student learning. The library is engaged in continuing renovation and identifying underused material that can be moved to offer more collaborative and quiet user space for its patrons." (*http://lib.utsa.edu/about/strategic-vision/2016/*)

University of Florida, George A. Smathers Libraries, Library West Library (http://www.uflib.ufl.edu/librarywest/; http://www.uflib.ufl.edu/)

General information about parent institution: The UF is a public land grant institution located in north central Florida. The student demographics reflect a diverse student population (data from ARL Statistics 2010):

- 31 616 undergraduates
- 18 211 graduates

How surveys were distributed: Bookmarks with a link and QR code to the survey were distributed by hand to students in the library along with a piece of chocolate candy. The distribution took place in the late afternoon and evening within the IC and on the sixth floor graduate area. For library staff, the Chair of Library West sent an email message briefly explaining the purpose of the survey with a link to access it. The email messages targeted staff that both work in the building and participate in serving on the reference desk in the IC, or at the circulation desk, or at the information point desk. In addition, the email included staff that work in other branch libraries or departments and volunteer to serve at these Library West service desks.

How the library will share survey results with customers and library staff: The authors will meet with the Library West staff to report selected information about student and library staff perceptions. After that meeting, the authors may write a brief article for the library newsletter and the faculty newsletter. Any changes to the layout of the IC as a direct consequence of the survey results will be highly publicized.

IC in renovated or new building: Library West was renovated with additional space added during 2004–06. The IC space on the third floor was an added attraction as well as a separate floor for graduate students only (sixth floor) and the Starbucks café on the first floor (*http://www.uflib.ufl.edu/librarywest/*).

Library information: George A. Smathers Libraries consist of the following libraries: Library West, Marston Science Library, Fine Arts & Architecture Library, Music Library, Education Library, Journalism & Communications Library, and Health Science Center Library. Together these libraries collaborate on digital collection purchases to advance access to research materials for the UF faculty and students. In addition, the libraries are active in the state consortia of the State University Library System (SUL) and regionals such as Association of Southeastern Research Libraries (ASERL) and Northeast Florida Library Information Network (NEFLIN), collaborating to expand and share collections with libraries within the state and in the southeastern region.

Library user survey: data and results

In this survey analysis users are defined as any student, teaching-faculty, researcher, institution staff, or visitor who was present in the library when the survey was distributed. Library participants reached out to users asking them to join in the survey by hand distributing flyers, through links to the survey on Facebook, Twitter, pop-ups on library websites, and working with student government to publicize and distribute the survey.

On the whole, the following evaluations are based on the combined responses from all five participating libraries unless otherwise stated.

The Library User Survey (Appendix A) consists of 17 questions, including the first question in which the participant voluntarily agrees to participate in the survey. From the five participating libraries, 1204 users agreed to participate in the survey for a response rate of 99 percent. Only nine respondents decided not to participate. The survey begins with questions that establish why the user comes to the library and concludes with demographic questions.

The second question asks the user "Why do you usually come into the library?" The question drew responses from 1148 participants who were asked to select up to three replies from 20 possible answers, including an "other" category, which instructed the respondent to add specific comments. The top three responses suggest that students are working on class assignments but first and foremost 84 percent agreed that they want a comfortable, quiet place to study. If they aren't studying quietly alone, slightly less than half of the respondents want to use computer workstations located in the library and collaborate with others on projects at a rate of 41.8 percent. The next three responses continue in the same vein demonstrating that library users are participating in the services that support their classwork and research assignments. They are taking care of business 40 percent of the time by checking out or renewing books, using a copier or scanner, accessing their email, and checking out course reserves.

Social activities that students might be involved in at the library appear mid-way down the ranked list of preferences. Serious study appears to take priority but getting a coffee and hanging out with friends, reserving a media room to collaborate on a project and using a computer for checking Facebook, Twitter or to take a break gaming and web browsing are all activities that rank higher in the users' perspective than consulting with library staff (22.6% to 16.5%).

What becomes evident when examining the ranked responses to this question is that users do not usually come into the library to seek assistance from librarians. The low-ranking, 4.4 percent to 2.4 percent, of such responses as "attend a class or workshop on library resources," "consult with a librarian about a class assignment or group project," and "consult with a librarian about my thesis or dissertation" verifies that students use the facility and the resources but are not aware of the subject specialties and research skills librarians have to offer them for class projects or assignments. We will discuss more findings about this question when we compare the user results with the library staff results later in this chapter.

After examining the comments recorded in the "other" category, the authors realized that the answer selection "use a copier or scanner" had an omission and should have included the term "printer" or have included a separate category for "printer" because 18 users commented that they come to the library specifically to print an assignment. Additional comments illustrate that students have reasons for coming to the library other than seeking a quiet place to study between classes, such as resting, using specific collections, taking advantage of the convenient location, and attending tutoring sessions.

In question 3, we ask the user to tell us if they access library services or resources from outside the library. Of the 1150 respondents, 70.9 percent of the users answered "yes" they do use library services remotely while only 29 percent replied "no" indicating that they do not access services or resources from outside the physical library. The "yes" respondents are asked two follow-up questions to clarify their positive response. With these two questions, we wanted to identify the type of technology students are using to get remote access and the variety of resources/services that they are accessing (Figure 6.1).

Out of the 798 respondents, 76.3 percent replying "yes" said that they access services or resources remotely using a laptop, tablet (iPad) or

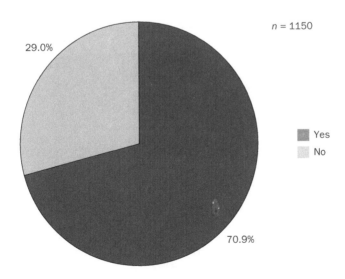

Figure 6.1 User Q3: Do you ever use Library Services or resources from outside the library?

netbook. Following mobile computer devices, 62.3 percent responded that they use their dorm or home desktop computer to access library resources remotely. Only 14.9 percent use their smartphones, from which we might surmise that the laptop/tablet computers are fast becoming the technology of choice for accessing library resources remotely. The screen size and the quick response-time of the larger portable equipment make tablets and netbooks much more conducive to searching and reading online than the smartphone (Figure 6.2).

Continuing on the remote access theme, the next question specifies the services or resources users are accessing from outside the library. Users were asked to select all that apply and their top choice at an impressive 70.5 percent is databases. The authors wonder if this is the result of good literacy training by librarians and professors or proof that users today are highly motivated self-starters. The next two selections garnering 43.7 percent and 35.1 percent respectively are logging into the library online catalog and into course reserves services to find and access research resources. Could these choices be interpreted as another sign that librarians and/or professors are reaching the students? Library online circulation services used for renewing or placing holds and interlibrary loan requests

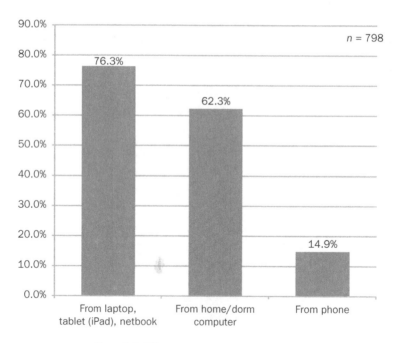

Figure 6.2   User Q4: When not in the library, how do you access services or resources? (Select all that apply)

are well-used online services ranking at 29 percent and 23.5 percent. Chat/instant messaging (IM)/Ask a Librarian services also received a double digit response rate but thereafter the rates drop to 7.2 percent or less confirming that library "how to get started" web pages and phone calls to the reference desk are not heavily used by students outside the library. From the "other" comments we learn that users are reserving rooms from an online reservation system/form. Pooling at the bottom of the list of services and resources, 2.8 percent or less, users are not accessing the library through social network services such as libraries' and librarians' Facebook, Twitter, or blog sites. Clearly students do not want to "network" with the library through any of the social media tools; rather, they prefer to come into the library for face-to-face contact with staff or receive replies to direct questions through chat or IM services (Figure 6.3).

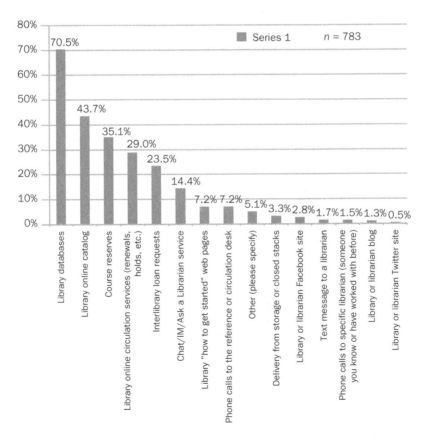

Figure 6.3 User Q5: What services or resources do you use from outside the library? (Select all that apply)

If the respondent answers "no," the survey directs them to explain why they don't use library services or resources from outside the library. Out of the 330 negative responders, 67 percent answered that they prefer to come into the library to access services or resources. Twenty percent of the responders voiced their frustration with remote access to library resources and selected the answer, "I have never figured out how to get to e-books, e-journals or library services from home." The "other" comments reveal 15 respondents that declared they have "no need" to access library resources or services from outside the library. The "no need" theme becomes more predominant later in the survey when participants are asked directly if they "ever ask library staff for help" (Figure 6.4).

The next question queries the user about how they start their research – the respondent may select up to three starting points. The authors also compare user responses with that of the library staff later in the chapter. Out of 1074 respondents, 66 percent of the users start their research project with Google. Wikipedia is the second preferred starting point with a response rate of 35 percent. The authors were not flummoxed by these replies; in fact, the responses confirm other survey and research

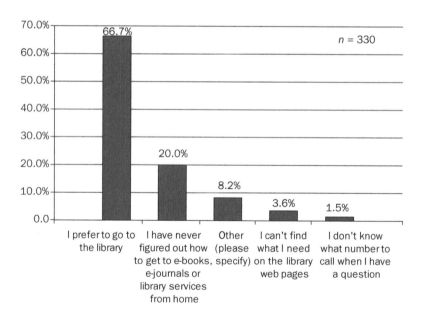

Figure 6.4 User Q6: Why don't you use library services or resources from outside the library?

findings in the literature. However, 31.4 percent responding "at the library catalog" was again an unexpected surprise and corresponds with the high regard for the online catalog found in the remote access questions earlier. The anthropological library studies covered in Chapter 4 disclosed that students look to their instructors for help. Indeed, the 30.5 percent response rate for preferring to consult with instructors or use course materials substantiates the trust students have in their professors' advice when beginning a research project. The results show that Google Scholar is the users' fifth choice as a starting point at a rate of 28 percent. The authors speculate about whether the users understand the difference between Google and Google Scholar and wonder if poor linking to full-text articles is the reason why they would not rank Google Scholar with its peer-reviewed sources over Google. In the "other" comments, 33 respondents indicated that they start their projects with databases – the authors realize that "databases" should have been included as a "starting point" answer and had it been included may have received a more remarkable response rate. "I ask a librarian for help" comes in at a weak 6 percent rate followed by even lower response rates for library subject guides, online library tutorials, library frequently asked questions (FAQ), and "how to get started" web pages (5% to 1%). "I ask my parents" falls into this group, which is a little puzzling and reveals a possible trend change in trusted authority figures from the anthropological studies of a few years ago. In those studies, students often displayed dependent behavior by frequently consulting with their parents about projects and preparing class assignments.

Responses to the question "When you come into the library, do you ever ask library staff for help with your research, for a class assignment" again expose and confirm what we have seen reported in other studies. Of the 1069 respondents, 47.3 percent replied that they never ask library staff for help. If the response was "never," the users were asked to comment on their response. Of the 506 who responded "never," 55 percent commented that they had "no need" for library staff assistance and 24 percent replied that they "didn't know" they could ask library staff for help, exhibiting that students don't have a clear understanding of the purpose or the function of librarians or library staff in the library. On the other hand, 46.9 percent respondents said that they ask for help "occasionally" but only 6 percent said that they ask for help "often." The authors see these results as telling signs of the divide between students and library staff. We question how librarians and library staff might counter the divide and re-establish their service role as trusted knowledge provider (Figures 6.5 and 6.6).

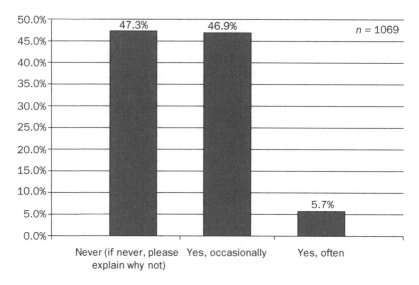

Figure 6.5 User Q8: **When you come to the library, do you ever ask library staff for help with your research, for a class assignment, etc.?**

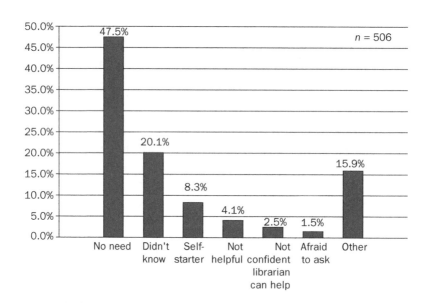

Figure 6.6 User Q8: Comments for (if never, please explain why not)

Juxtaposed against the above question, the authors continue to wonder about the users' thought process as they responded to the question, "When you have a library reference or service question, how do you prefer to contact the library?" The users could select up to three preferences and the overwhelming favorite was "in-person at public desk" at a high rate of 77 percent out of the 1073 responders. Email followed at 27 percent and voice phone at 19 percent round out the top three choices, showing that the respondents prefer personal attention when they do have questions. Their responses demonstrate that even if they do not fully understand what library staff is there for, they want personal service when they are in need. "I never contact the library" at a rate of 13 percent shows that some respondents think of themselves as "self-starters" and will look elsewhere for assistance when and if they ever require help. "Chat/IM" at a rate of 11 percent again illustrates that users want personal assistance at the point of need; however, they are not so enamored with personal assistance that they will make an office consultation appointment with a librarian – this response received a rate of only 5 percent. The remaining responses as well as comments in the "other" category continue to show users' lack of interest in using social network tools for seeking help or communicating with library staff.

Nevertheless, library staff should feel somewhat gratified by the significant number that selected positive replies when asked how they perceive library staff. With up to three selections, "generally helpful" topped the users' assessment of library staff at 80.2 percent out of 1070 respondents to the question. After that fine yet nonspecific endorsement, the percentage of selected responses dropped appreciably with participants finding library staff helpful for research problems (18.8%), as advisors or consultants (17.5%), technical problems assistants (16.3%), content providers (15.6%), and last and somewhat disappointing as instructors (13.9%). So in general, users find library staff helpful overall, offering directions, locating a resource either in the stacks or online, and checking out or renewing materials. Yet for specific tasks or problems, users do not seem to consider library staff as reliable or do not even realize the extensive skills library staff has to offer. Toward the bottom of the spectrum, the respondents see library staff as "irrelevant – can find all I need online without a librarian's help" (4.5%) and only 3 percent believe that library staff has knowledge of or expertise in Internet/technology. These last two answers are reflected in the comments of the "other" category (5%), in which users state that they find staff "not helpful," "rude," and "not confident librarian can help." Although the users overwhelmingly describe library staff as "generally helpful," there is a recurring theme in the comments that student assistants are not the preferred choice for help: "Every time I go to the library it looks like they have students working behind the desk, and I don't really trust them to give me any useful advice." Further analysis should disclose how divided perceptions actually are when the authors compare the library staff's response to this same question with that of the users' responses.

The library facility question fares well with 1074 respondents identifying the library as a "clean well-lighted place" where they can find comfortable furniture and personal or group study space. However, the comments penned by students for this question show some dissatisfaction and name inadequacies for: the number of computers, individual study space, space in general during peak times, outlets for personal electronics, group study space, and tables and seating in general. The authors will discuss and compare the very different perceptions voiced by users and library staff about the facility later in the chapter.

The user status question attracted 1121 respondents from all class levels but the undergraduate status at 84 percent by far monopolized the respondent numbers. Graduates responded at the rate of 8 percent and Post-Bac at the low rate of 1 percent. These results reflect that undergraduates appear to be the predominant users of Information/ Learning Commons areas in libraries and value the services and resources of these humanities and social science collections. Of the 1040 users responding to the question asking about off-campus or on-campus residence, most, 64 percent, live off-campus. Only 36 percent live on-campus and because of that proximity probably have greater or easier access to the library. On the other hand, users living off-campus might be inclined to take advantage of remote access to databases because traveling into the library may not be as convenient for them. This is speculation and would have to be tested with more pointed questions. The same may be true for room reservations – it would be interesting to see if there is a correlation between living off campus and the use of online reservations for study rooms. Plus it would be another way to gauge the "convenience is king" factor. A close examination of the staff survey should disclose differences in research approach and behavior between users and library staff. More telling will be the areas that reveal similar points-of-view – do we have enough behavioral information to make educated conjectures?

Library staff survey: data and results

The authors asked the partner librarians to get as large a staff sample size as possible, realizing that staff sizes and library organization would determine the pool of respondents. Library staff is defined as librarians, library administrators, paraprofessional staff, and student staff working in the library and receiving the request to respond to the survey through email or print handouts. Some of the library contacts discussed the surveys at staff meetings. Most distributed them via email, some to the entire library staff; others took a more targeted approach to the public services staff only. Sample sizes at each library ranged from a low of 25 to a high of 62 for a total of 214 staff responses.

For purposes of this analysis, the following statements will most often relate to the total combined responses of all participant libraries unless otherwise specified. Staff responses were remarkably similar across all libraries, except in the case of a few questions for which it is useful to discuss notable differences between locations. The comparison questions will be analyzed more fully at the end of the chapter to compare the perceptions of library users and library staff.

The first question of the 19-question Library Staff Survey (Appendix B) is the acceptance of the described research and the respondent's voluntary acceptance of the terms of participation. All five partner libraries experienced at least a few drop-outs immediately after acceptance but two libraries have much higher percentages of staff suspending participation. Some of the more complex questions elicited lower response rates from participants, again across all five libraries.

The second question asks the staff respondent to select from a list of service modes all that apply to their job duties. The common denominator is service via voice phone for almost 70 percent of the respondents. The online forms of reference ("virtual or chat reference; email reference") come in at second place at four out of the five libraries. All five libraries still report some kind of "reference or research desk" activity, making it third place in the overall ranking, but less than half ($n = 75$) of the 163 respondents to this question serve there. The highest percentages of in-person desk work are from Library A where reportedly there is a desk service expectation written into a majority of public service job descriptions as well as a number of staff members working mainly behind the scenes who choose to volunteer for one or two hours per week at a public desk. Library B has a particularly low rate (21.7%) of participation at the reference desk and a correspondingly high percentage of staff (52.2%) engaging in office consultations. Overall, the choices for the circulation and information desks were chosen by a significant percentage (over 25%) of respondents as well, demonstrating the staff-intensive nature of the in-person desk services at all libraries. Reference via phone texting is clearly not yet established in four out of five of the participant libraries and library staff assignments to the "technical support desk" are low or nonexistent at all libraries. In the "other" comments, four respondents at Library D mentioned providing services at an academic departmental library and another respondent wrote of their information literacy work with academic faculty. "Reference via social media" as an assignment is also mentioned once in the open comments (Figure 6.7).

"How do you serve the patrons?" is the third survey question; respondents could choose up to three functions they most perform. Only one person indicated no contact with the patrons at all. "Answer reference questions" was one of the top three picks for 69 percent of the total sample, seemingly contradictory to reports in the literature of declining reference activity and interesting in that this activity is not necessarily connected to a high rate of participation at a reference or research desk in all libraries. "Directional assistance" was the next highest choice for 53 percent of the respondents. "Help students with class assignments" comes in next, followed by consultations and referrals. Library B is the one departure from this order, demonstrating a vital research assistance program with higher percentages of consultations and class assignment support over directional assistance and despite a low rate of participation in a traditional reference desk environment. Library A has a notably higher percentage (46%) of respondents who provide circulation duties ("check out or renew materials") but no participation in the survey by student assistants, leading the authors to assume a higher than normal assignment of regular staff to circulation duties. "Check out laptop or other equipment" is notable only at Library A as well. "Assistance with copiers, scanners, or printers" was chosen by 26 percent of the total sample, but "computer (hardware and software) assistance" was lower than the authors expected; below 10 percent for three libraries but around 20 percent for the other two libraries. It would be interesting to correlate percentage of technical questions with the existence of an IT support desk in the library and IT staff providing patron assistance. Some "other" patron duties include retrieving and locating materials, dealing with facilities problems, contacting potential donors, and answering questions about catalog problems.

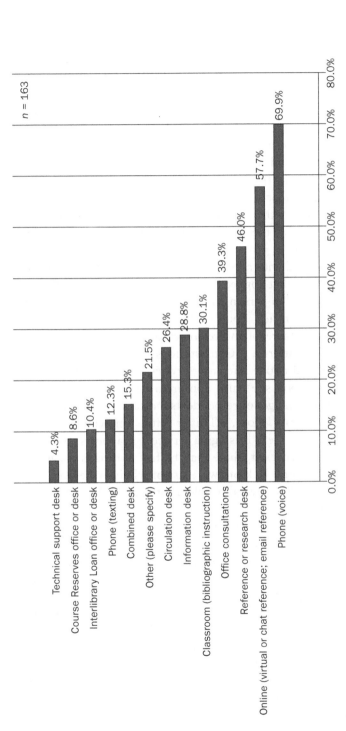

Figure 6.7 Staff Q2: In your current library position, where do you serve the library patrons? (Select all that apply)

Staff respondents next chose up to three reasons why they think most students come to the library. This is one of the user/staff comparison questions that will be more fully analyzed later in this chapter. "Comfortable, quiet place to study" is the top rated choice at 62 percent of the staff sample, but "use a computer workstation ..." and "collaborate with others on a project" come in quite closely at second and third place. Thirty-six percent of the staff think that use of a computer workstation in the IC for personal and social reasons (Facebook, gaming, shopping, etc.) is very likely one of the students' main reasons for coming to the library. "Check out or renew books" was chosen by 23.5 percent of the sample. One of the "other" respondents noted the existence and popularity of tutoring at the library and supplemental instruction for writing center support.

The survey continued with a list of types of assistance from which the respondents picked all that applied to the services their library offers. As expected, some type of "in-person service at public desks" is provided by all five participant libraries; none of the participating libraries have indicated complete closure of the reference desk although some have altered scheduling patterns. "Consultations with librarians/subject specialists," email and phone reference services, "chat or IM services," and a "library Facebook site" also appear to be universal to the five libraries. Smaller percentages of respondents indicate their knowledge of the existence of "library blogs," Twitter sites, "individual librarian Facebook sites," and a "text messaging service." It appears that where these services do indeed exist, there may be few librarians engaged in providing service and/or a lack of awareness of relatively new and non-traditional service models. Several people mentioned "subject guides" in the "other" comments.

The next two questions were a bit more complicated and were intended to measure staff preferences for the types of reference service they most like to perform versus the types of reference service the staff feels must be maintained "when resources are scarce." The number of respondents who skipped these two questions was higher than for the rest of the survey, perhaps because they take time to consider and rank. The authors conjecture that if taken seriously, these questions also require some difficult choices that librarians don't really like to consider. Over 50 percent ($n = 71$) of the respondents place "in-person service at public desks" as their top ranked choice for providing reference assistance; no other modes come close to this percentage. Combining ranks 1–4 brings "in-person service ..." to 82.2 percent of the sample. "Email" is at second place with 75.7 percent of the sample choosing it somewhere within ranks 1–4. "Office consultations" were placed in the top four ranks by 67.2 percent of the respondents. Library B and Library C show strong support for office consultations: 50 percent making consultations their first choice at Library B and 52.6% of Library C respondents ranking consultations at second place. Text reference via phone is not favored at this point in time. The authors were surprised that "chat/IM" reference is not favored at any library; only five people (3.6 percent) put it as their first choice and 40 percent place it in ranks 1–4. The lack of enthusiasm for chat reference is interesting given the evidence from many libraries that the electronic means of reference assistance are experiencing increases in activity and complexity of questions while in-person reference has dramatically decreased (see Chapter 2 and Radford, 2008). However, survey respondents at least favor chat over the social media as a means of reference service (blogs, Facebook, and Twitter.) One person tells us how they really feel, stating emphatically, "I prefer *not* to perform reference in Facebook, Twitter, Text, or Blogs" and eight others express similar sentiments in the "other" comments.

When faced with resource challenges, the library staff across all five libraries again designate "in-person service at public desks" as their number one choice for services to retain, giving it even more votes at 60.8 percent ($n = 90$) of the sample. Combining ranks 1–4, just a few people decided that placing in-person reference in the top tier would be unwise during difficult times, dropping from 82.2 percent favorability to 79.1 percent. "Office consultations" again rate highly with 65.6 percent placing it in ranks 1–4, dead even with email and only slightly edging out voice phone at 65.5 percent. Attitudes towards modes of reference change only when we get past the top four modes: in-person, email, office consultations, and voice phone. Chat/IM reference comes up a full 10 percent in favorability when resources are scarce. Reference via phone texting also moves up almost 10 percent as though it would be taken more seriously should staff resources dwindle. Facebook and Twitter again barely register, even in difficult times, with blogs receiving just a few more votes as the fifth or sixth choice to retain. In the "other" comments, one person made the practical point that the library should "shift services to evening" when resources are scarce. Another mentioned appointments as an option to scheduling the reference desk at all times (Figure 6.8).

Later in this chapter, the authors will compare the students' answers to a similar question that explores how they prefer to contact library staff when needing assistance with a "library reference or service question."

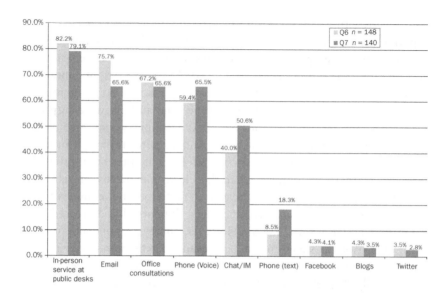

Figure 6.8 Staff Q6: When I perform Reference services I prefer ...;
Staff Q7: When resources are scarce, what Reference
services should be offered? (Ranks 1–4 used)

The eighth question asks the library staff to indicate the resources (up to three) they most often advise to patrons starting their research. The top four choices were: (1) 66.9 percent start "at the library home page"; (2) 49.7 percent at "library subject guides"; (3) 46.4 percent start with a "reference interview"; (4) 34.4 percent "at the library catalog." Of the 18 percent who indicated "other" responses, a significant number of respondents mentioned the Summon Discovery OneSearch service. The authors neglected to specify either discovery or meta-search engines as a choice. These tools streamline the research process and it's clear they will be an increasingly important starting point for research. As expected, the "Google" and "Wikipedia" choices received few votes from the staff, although "Google Scholar" did get almost 11 percent of the vote. Only 13 people indicated referrals to a subject specialist as one of their top three starting points, possibly indicating that general reference is strong at all five libraries. Very few start in either the reference collection or by giving the user "a call number section to browse." Finally, the bottom two choices are the "online library tutorials" (four respondents) and the "library FAQ" (one respondent). It is clear from the responses to this question that the library's web presence, whether starting at the library catalog, the subject guides, the discovery service, or somewhere else on the home page, is extremely important to the librarians who are instructing patrons in how to begin their research. Later in this chapter, the authors will compare the staff responses to this question to the user responses to a similar question. Not unexpectedly, the users take very different approaches to research, but there were also some surprising similarities.

The library staff was next asked, "How do you think most patrons perceive library staff in your institution?" Respondents were asked to select up to three descriptive phrases. The responses to this question are also targeted as one of the authors' comparisons to be discussed later in this chapter. We feel it is particularly important to understand how the increasingly self-sufficient students view the role of the library staff. The majority of respondents (80.9 percent) feel the students perceive library staff as "generally helpful." No other response came close to this top choice but "helpful for research problems" and "content provider – getting them what they need or want" followed, respectively, at nearly 44 percent and 39 percent. Over 20 percent of the staff respondents feel that students find library staff to be "irrelevant" – are these librarians feeling pessimistic, or just being realistic? The authors will try to answer that question when we look at the user responses to this question. Almost 9 percent perceive students as impatient with getting "too much information."

The tenth survey question asks staff to describe their library facility by means of nine questions that query the adequacy (yes or no) of certain features of the building. These questions are repeated in the user survey and will be discussed in more detail in the comparison section of this chapter. Overall, the responses from the library staff are more critical of the facility than those of the users. As a companion to this information, the authors worked with Carrico and Lindell to design a more detailed question (number 13) that rates specific library areas, including the staff work spaces. Carrico and Lindell analyze the results for the facilities questions in detail in Chapter 3 of this book.

Questions 11 and 12 ask about the status of the respondent's library: has it "undergone a large renovation or added/remodeled space ..." or is it a new library "built in the past five years?" All five participating libraries have some renovated space and one library has a new library building on campus. For each of these questions, only 4 percent of the respondents did not know if their building was renovated or new. The authors attribute this lack of knowledge either to being new staff and/or to uncertainty over the exact date of renovation or construction.

The staff survey continues with some demographic questions that track the positions of the responding library staff members, years in their present position, and years in the library profession. Over half of the 146 respondents are in "permanent staff positions." Most of the libraries received responses from fairly equal numbers of paraprofessional staff members and professional "librarians," presumably reflecting the overall composition of their staff; however, Library C has a proportionately smaller number of librarians and in fact noted a number of staffing cuts and unfilled librarian positions. Only Library E obtained "student employee" responses; this is unfortunate given the likelihood that all five libraries have students working in public service positions, especially during nights and weekends. Only nine administrators across all libraries participated in the survey (Figure 6.9).

The number of years the respondents have been in the library profession validates the much discussed "greying of the profession." Fifty-two percent of the 154 respondents have been in the profession more than 10 years and almost half of those for "21 or more years."

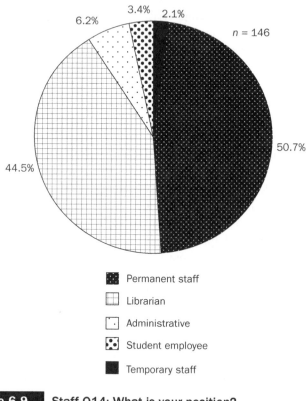

Permanent staff

Librarian

Administrative

Student employee

Temporary staff

Figure 6.9   **Staff Q14: What is your position?**

While the authors feel that generational differences are over-hyped in the literature, it is worth noting that preferences are no doubt affected by history and the longer view of change through time. Although all five libraries have staff members who have been in their present position more than 20 years, there is also significant movement and new hiring. Over 50% of the respondents have been in their present position five years or fewer (Figures 6.10 and 6.11).

The survey concludes with two questions that address user feedback mechanisms. Most of the staff (71.5%) indicated that their library "conducts user surveys." One library was on the low end of the scale with only 50% indicating they knew of the existence of surveys. Nearly 23 percent overall had no idea whether their library did surveys or not. When asked about other means of feedback, including "focus group discussions and interviews with users," 34.8 percent did not know. Library D had fewer people indicating they did not know, but a split

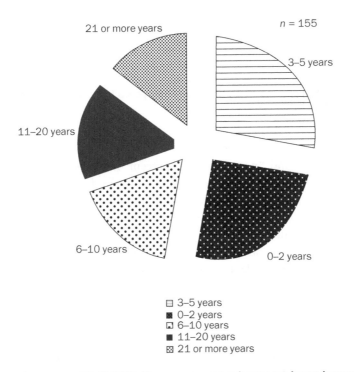

3–5 years	
0–2 years	
6–10 years	
11–20 years	
21 or more years	

Figure 6.10 Staff Q15: How many years have you been in your present position?

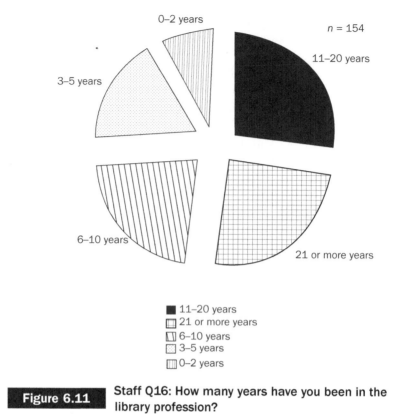

0–2 years

3–5 years

11–20 years

n = 154

6–10 years

21 or more years

■ 11–20 years
▥ 21 or more years
▨ 6–10 years
▦ 3–5 years
▥ 0–2 years

Figure 6.11 Staff Q16: How many years have you been in the library profession?

between "yes" and "no." Sixty-five percent of the people in Library B did not know if focus groups or interviews were done. Clearly, either a small group is handling user feedback initiatives in the five libraries, or little is being done, but either way the rest of the staff remains largely uninformed (Figure 6.12).

The two surveys show some interesting trends and contradictions when examined on their own, but the authors were certain that illuminating similarities and differences would be seen with a comparative analysis of staff and user responses for identical or very similarly constructed questions. The comparative nature of the surveys is what makes the authors' study unique and provides a jumping-off point for further research. The analysis will also comprise part of the authors' call for action to bridge the divide.

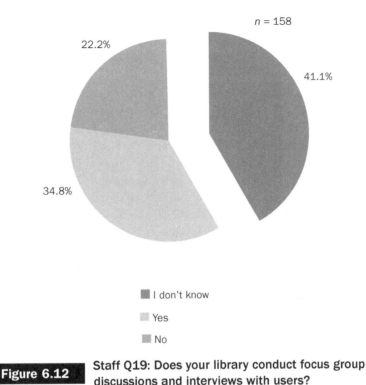

n = 158

22.2%

41.1%

34.8%

■ I don't know

▨ Yes

▨ No

Figure 6.12 Staff Q19: Does your library conduct focus group discussions and interviews with users?

Library users and library staff: how they compare

Why two surveys? In order to examine and compare user and library staff perceptions about services and space in the IC, we developed similar questions and included them in the surveys for both groups. Our intention was to find out what was working within the IC while exploring perceptions that users and library staff have about each other and the library. We discovered common threads in our surveys with that of usage/satisfaction evaluations in recent anthropological library studies and user experience interviews – namely, users do not understand the tasks librarians/library staff perform and users' need for librarian assistance continues to decline. As with the analysis earlier in this chapter, evaluations are based on the combined responses from all five participating libraries unless otherwise stated. In addition, a closer look at the comments derived from both surveys provides elucidatory insight regarding user and library staff perceptions of the library as place.

The users and library staff were asked to select up to three answers for the first comparison questions "why do you usually come into the library" and "why do you think students usually come into the library." The responses reveal that library users and staff across all five libraries selected the same responses as their top three choices. The three choices are as follows: "comfortable quiet place to study," "use a computer workstation for a class assignment," and "collaborate with others on a project." A close examination of the library staff's selection of that same response shows that Library B respondents think that "use a computer for a class assignment" is equal to "comfortable quiet place to study" giving both answers response rates of 56.5 percent. Libraries D and E both selected the response "use a computer workstation for a class assignment" as their top choice but when combined with the responses of the other libraries "use a computer workstation ..." drops to second place overall. "Collaborate with others on a project" also shows slight variation for library staff and library users with some libraries showing a preference for "collaborate with others" as their second top reason for coming into the library. In the next four responses, library staff and users differ insignificantly in their preferences. Users' selections indicate that they are all business when they come to the library, choosing "check out or renew books," "use a copier or scanner," "check email," and "use course reserves." Library staff respondents selected "use a computer workstation for personal/social activities" as their fourth response indicating that they think students come to the library to look at their Facebook or Twitter accounts, or play games or web browsing rather than engaging in academic activities. In fact, the users select this choice as tenth in their preference list. Tenth on the library staff list is "consulting with a librarian about a class assignment," which appears much lower on the users' list of reasons for coming to the library. The authors think that the responses recorded for this question illustrate that users and library staff experience a divide in their perceptions because librarians do not recognize the sincerity of the users' focus on studying. Indeed, as Figure 6.13 illustrates, users' top reasons for being in the library are to study alone or to collaborate with a group but usually not to consult with librarians. On the other hand, library staff has not truly registered this sentiment because librarians selected the "consult with a librarian

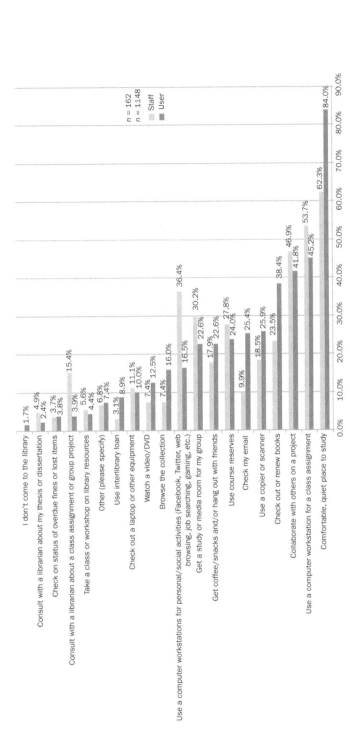

Figure 6.13 Staff Q4: Why do you think most patrons come into the library? (Select up to 3); User Q2: Why do you usually come into the library? (Select up to 3)

about a class assignment" at a significantly higher percentage than the users did. We suspect that library staff is still holding out hope for some change that will bring the users back to the reference desk asking for help. The "other" category did not reveal any insights into users' reasoning for not seeking librarian or staff assistance when they are in the library. However, the library users' comments divulge an oversight on the part of the authors in not clearly stating "printer" as an option in the "use a copier or scanner" response. Eighteen users commented that they come to the library specifically to use the printers. Whereas, the library staff comments record only one comment about "printer" usage.

In the next question users are asked how they start their research and staff is asked how it advises users to start their research; both surveys asked the respondents to select up to three starting points. The answer selections are the same for both groups. "Google" by far is the place where users begin their research and "Wikipedia" is next with the "library catalog" following close behind. The authors expected "Google" and "Wikipedia" to rank high for users but never expected "library catalog" to rank in their top three choices. Conversely, library staff favored "at the library home page" as the top choice, ranking it slightly higher than "Google" ranked for the user. "Library subject guides" and "reference interviews" rank as close second and third choices for library staff. The responses provided by these two groups may suggest the methodology that each exercises when starting or advising how to start a research project. However, a closer look at the apparent divergence in approach illustrates the divide between librarians/library staff and library users. When librarians start research assistance "at the library home page," perhaps they believe they are selecting this option because it offers the user a number of tools that could help them form a search strategy for locating appropriate research resources. The user does not even consider that option until seventh down their list. The authors speculate that users probably do not know how to or desire to navigate through the many choices on most library home pages; rather, users exhibit through their responses a direct approach and go to the "library catalog" (their third choice) to find resources the library owns. Indeed, users responded that they are searching specific databases when they commented in the "other" category tenth down on their list. Library staff also specified "databases" in the "other" category, fifth on its list, but at a significantly lower rate than users. Library staff also mentioned "discovery services" in this category – both of these answers should have been included in the question selections and is an admitted oversight on the part of the authors. The fourth response for both groups is interesting because it reveals more about the research methodology of both groups. Users initially take a broad approach with "Google" and "Wikipedia" and then turn to the library resources through a library catalog search. At this point, when they cannot find what they need, they turn to their instructor or use course materials. On the other hand, librarians take the tried and true approach staying with the native tools such as the "library subject guides" and "reference interviews" before moving on to the "library catalog." They resort to the broad view of "Google Scholar" and then "Google" as their sixth and seventh choice on the list of possibilities. As noted in the user analysis earlier, students do not use the "library subject guides," "online tutorials," "library FAQ," or "how to get started Web pages," which fall to the bottom of their selection list. Users rank "ask a librarian for help" as ninth on their list of 16 choices – verifying that users trust their professors and classmates for research advice much more than librarians or their parents (14 on their list). For librarians/library staff, "Wikipedia," "online tutorials," and "library FAQ" fall to the bottom of the list and cause the authors to wonder if the time spent on designing and creating tutorials, how to get started web pages or FAQs are really worth the effort if users are not accessing the material and librarians appear to dismiss them as impracticable tools (Figure 6.14).

The two questions above emphasize how students and staff interact with library resources; the next question focuses on what students think about librarian/library staff as they interact with them in the library. We asked users to tell us "how do you perceive library staff" and library staff "how do you think most patrons perceive library staff"; each group selected up to three responses. Both groups believe that library staff is "generally helpful" with percentage rates registering remarkable agreement, recording users at 80.2 percent and library staff at 80.9 percent. In general users seem to think librarians are helpful for assisting with research and/or technical problems or they view library staff as advisors/consultants. The librarians/library staff think users see them as "helpful for research problems," "content provider," and "instructor." However, librarians/library staff experiencing loneliness at the reference desk responded that patrons see them as irrelevant midway down their list. Users on the other hand ranked that point-of-view farther down their list at 10 but did rank N/A ("I never interact with library staff") as seventh on the list. Typically, the "other" category divulges some insights and in this case negative responses. Some users commented that library staff is

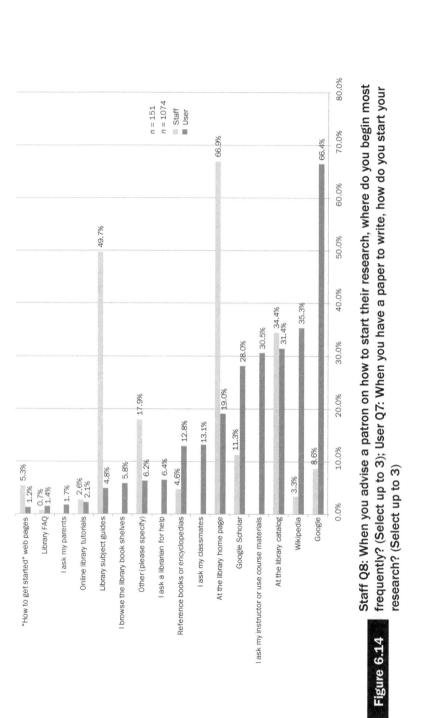

Figure 6.14 Staff Q8: When you advise a patron on how to start their research, where do you begin most frequently? (Select up to 3); User Q7: When you have a paper to write, how do you start your research? (Select up to 3)

Chart data (left to right categories):

Category	Staff	User
"How to get started" web pages	1.2%	5.3%
Library FAQ	0.7%	1.4%
I ask my parents		1.7%
Online library tutorials	2.6%	2.1%
Library subject guides	49.7%	4.8%
I browse the library book shelves		5.8%
Other (please specify)	17.9%	6.2%
I ask a librarian for help		6.4%
Reference books or encyclopedias	4.6%	12.8%
I ask my classmates		13.1%
At the library home page	66.9%	19.0%
Google Scholar	11.3%	28.0%
I ask my instructor or use course materials		30.5%
At the library catalog	34.4%	31.4%
Wikipedia	3.3%	35.3%
Google	8.6%	66.4%

n = 151 Staff
n = 1074 User

"unhelpful," "rude," and they are "not confident that librarians can help them." Other remarks about librarians appearing "too busy to help" or "too engaged with other librarians" to answer questions show that students have experienced some unapproachable behavior when venturing to the reference desk for help (Figure 6.15).

The authors have provided an in-depth look at the staff preferences for reference service, contrasting how librarians prefer to serve the public with what they think priorities should be during difficult economic times, or as we phrased it in the survey, "when resources are scarce." In truth, there is little change in the responses between the two questions, except for a subtle shift when resources are scarce toward chat reference and the phone, whether texting or traditional voice phone reference. When we ask the users how they prefer to contact us with reference or service questions, we get answers remarkably similar to ours. The users were asked to indicate up to three preferences for contacting the library; in the interests of keeping the user survey simple and short, we did not ask them to rank as we did the staff. Almost 77 percent of the users prefer "in-person service at public desks." This figure is perplexing, given other data the authors have presented in this chapter. Over 47 percent of the surveyed users, the vast majority of which are students, never ask library staff for help, either because they don't need us, do not know that we are available for help, or prefer not to ask for various reasons. Yet they want the library staff to be there. Although perplexing, this is not the first time we have heard about this seeming contradiction. Just like the librarians, the users do not favor "IM/chat"; slightly over 10 percent put it in their three preferences. However, as the authors stated earlier in the chapter, student use of chat goes up every year. The users join the library staff in their preference for email and voice phone and they like phone texting only slightly more than the library staff does (2.5% of users to 1.4% of staff declaring texting to be their top choice.) Although generational studies have declared email to be dead to the students, the authors believe this not to be the case. The students use email for business, just as does the library staff but they have not extended their high use of texting to the library; texting is for communicating with friends and family, not librarians. The biggest divergence between library staff and users occurs with respect to office consultations. The authors surmise that the users are either unaware of the possibility of office consultations with librarians or have no interest. Only 5 percent of the user respondents picked the consultation option,

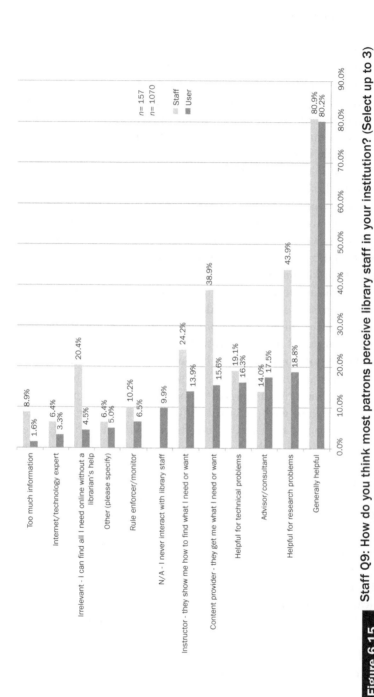

Figure 6.15 Staff Q9: How do you think most patrons perceive library staff in your institution? (Select up to 3)
User Q10: In general, how do you perceive library staff? (Select up to 3)

whereas over 67 percent of the library staff places it in the ranked top tier of choices. As reference desks close and when in-person service is curtailed, the library staff needs to be mindful of the lack of user awareness of the existence and value of consultations.

Both users and staff answered a multi-part question that provided a simple yes or no response to assess their satisfaction with particular building features. It is easy to see from a quick glance at the chart (Figure 6.16) that the responses from the library staff are more critical of the facility than those of the users. This is not surprising given the familiarity with which the library staff views the building day in and day out. In addition, library staff must deal with the facilities problems and complaints of the users. Carrico and Lindell also noted in Chapter 3 the feeling among staff at the libraries they surveyed that staff concerns and suggestions were not heard when planning for renovations and new buildings, an attitude that would certainly affect their view of the facilities. The negative responses of the library staff are significantly higher in every category, but the point of departure is most evident with the question that covers adequacy of staffing. The number of staff concerned with the staffing levels at their libraries is high across all five libraries, never dropping below 30 percent and reaching a high of 86.1 percent at Library C. Few students express the need for more staff; 5.7 percent ($n = 61$) of the 1074 respondents answered negatively to the adequacy of staffing. It is a testament to the library staff that students are not complaining about long lines and wait times. Neither do they take issue with where the service desks are located. However, we have to take this news with a grain of salt because the users have also told us loudly and clearly that they do not need or want our help. If they are not really looking for us, chances are they won't miss us. The users also have no concept of the long hours spent at the desk. They have noted in their comments that library staff members are sometimes crabby or unapproachable, but may not connect this with long hours and lack of staff.

As noted in the staff data section, the safety of all five library buildings receives very good reviews. In fact, students are even more enthusiastic, 95.8 percent of them feeling "safe and secure." The users also are far less concerned about cleanliness (users 93.7% positive, staff 66.5% positive), leading to the assumption that the libraries are indeed "clean and inviting" because the staff is vigilant about it. Where there is the most meeting of the minds with respect to the facilities is with the concern for space needs. Over and over again in the open

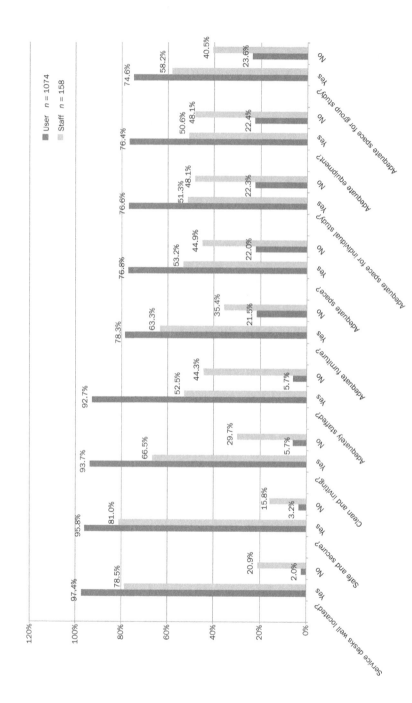

Figure 6.16 User Q11 and Staff Q10: What do you think of the present library facility?

comments, the students mention lack of computers, worse at Library C than all other libraries, as does the staff. Individual study space and quiet study space versus group study space is also a common theme among both students and staff. Both groups mention the crowds at peak times of the year. The students complain more about the lack of outlets for their laptops than do the librarians. The users want more comfortable furniture, while the librarians seem to express more concern about deteriorating and badly designed furniture. It is clear from the building comparisons that there is understanding between the two groups about the major building concerns such as space. The statistics show that the librarians are aware and conflicted about the competing needs of quiet space or group space and have the same concerns about over-crowding and lack of computers at peak usage times. The greatest divide comes from the very different viewpoints of the librarians, who see the traffic flow and long standing problems, whether cleaning, staffing, or furniture design, and the students, who mostly want comfort and convenience while they are there but don't think about long-term implications.

Review of findings and comments

We don't have to worry about getting people into the library – they are there! Many libraries are reporting record-setting gate counts after instituting new ICs or renovating buildings. But the Crump/Freund survey showed that the greatest divide occurs with the large percentage of the respondents who do not even know what we do as librarians and approach research with a self-reliance born of their facility with the Internet. When asked if they ever go to library staff for help, 506 people said "never" and were asked to explain why not. The coded comments included 330 respondents who basically said they had no need or were self-starters. A total of 119 did not know they had the option to ask us for help. Twenty-four of the respondents said the library staff is not helpful.

For many, we are simply not needed:

> "I don't have many research papers to do and it is easier for me to do them by myself."

"I don't know what I'm supposed to ask them about. I think I would come to them if I had a question I couldn't google, but that hardly ever happens."

Or feel they should be able to do without us:

"If you need help from a librarian, then your high school teachers failed you in the paper-writing department."

"... I'm a big boy, I can do it myself."

Some have little confidence in us:

"Don't expect them to know the details about my class assignment. They would probably give help that is vague."

"I don't usually find they are very helpful. I wish they were."

Others have no clue:

"I just didn't know I should do that."

"I didn't know that they were allowed to help with research."

Some can't be bothered:

"I'm too lazy, just want to get the paper/assignment done."

"I do my research at my apartment."

And others try to make us feel better:

"I've never really thought about it, but I must admit it would be advantageous."

"I don't like wasting time with a question when I know if I work hard enough, I can figure it out myself... I'm very independent... but library staff are generally very nice and helpful."

For the most part, they like us, but is that enough? As a profession, do we settle for being "generally helpful"? Are we willing to give up our traditional role, our organizational structure, and our legacy processes to truly engage with the individual user and devote ourselves to their needs?

References

Adhami, N. (2011). *Post-occupancy evaluation of Library West's interior design: A method to explore pre-design research and programming* [master's thesis]. Retrieved from UF Online Dissertations database: *http://purl.fcla.edu/fcla/etd/UFE0042985*

Barratt, C. C., Acheson, P., & Luken, E. (2010). Reference models in the electronic library: The Miller Center at the University of Georgia. *Reference Services Review, 38*(1), 44–56. DOI: 10.1108/00907321011020716

Radford, M. L. (2008). A personal choice: Reference service excellence. *Reference & User Services Quarterly, 48*(2), 108, 110–115. Retrieved from *http://rusa.metapress.com/content/L74261/*

7

Reaching across the divide

Michele J. Crump and LeiLani S. Freund

Abstract: The concluding chapter examines the distinctive aspects of the Crump/Freund survey assessment within the context of the information commons (IC). The authors validate their unique approach through reviewing other survey studies, showing how their look at library users and library staff across five academic libraries reveals a common divide between user and librarian. The study confirms that IC librarians and staff need to find a way to brand services and expertise to remain viable in the collaborative setting. The chapter confirms the necessity for communication on all levels with faculty, students, and library staff alike – communication that invites ongoing dialogue, fosters trust, and promotes community within the academy. In their final words, the authors emphasize that through partnership with the library user librarians just might bridge the divide.

Key words: academic community, information commons (IC), learning commons, librarian perceptions, librarian survey, student perceptions, user experience, user survey.

"… but when I went to school I observed a number of ways in which the industrious teacher of English could ignore the nature of literature, but continue to teach the subject."

– F. O'Connor (1979) *Mystery and manners; Occasional prose, selected & edited by Sally and Robert Fitzgerald*, p. 125

"We are putting our focus squarely on the user and presenting the library as a platform for 'getting academic projects done,' providing appropriate tools, and stepping aside."

– S. Kennedy (2011) Farewell to the reference librarian.

Concluding words

When the authors embarked on this research project, we wanted to find out three things: Is there a true divide between students and library staff concerning library services and library as place? Is the information commons (IC) working to help close the assumed divide? Would comparing library user and staff perceptions offer insights about how libraries can better address the research needs of library patrons? We immediately thought that comparing survey results between library staff and library users' perceptions from several academic institutions would tell us if a true divide does indeed exist. We did not want to simply repeat earlier studies; instead, we created the two surveys to appraise perspectives concerning services, environment, and customer interaction. In our literature search we did not locate a study that surveyed and compared the perceptions of library staff and library patrons. Rather, we found glimmers of library staff perspectives on services, patrons, and library as place in anecdotal and formal interviews performed during anthropological library studies, some of which are reviewed in Chapter 4 of this publication and not revisited here. Another unique factor in our study is the inclusion of the IC in the service equation. The authors believe that our survey results produce an honest look at the IC in academic libraries by explaining what is working and what is not.

Comparable to the Crump/Freund study, the University of Sheffield Library survey conducted by Rachel Bickley and Sheila Corrall (2011) is a unique study that makes some pertinent observations about student perceptions of library staff in the IC. Bickley and Corrall believe their study to be the first UK survey to query students' perceptions about librarians in an IC setting. Their findings record results that coincide with earlier surveys tracking perceptions – students do not visit the IC for help; students have a general positive perception about library staff; negative experiences with staff inhibit patron's "subsequent use of enquiry"; librarians' expertise is underutilized (Bickley & Corrall, 2011, pp. 236–237). With the focus on IC, Bickley and Corrall (2011) show that even though the collaborative facilities provide a one-stop service point, "the proliferation of services and the combination of physical and virtual learning environments have complicated matters" and often confuse users looking for assistance (p. 239). Corresponding to the Crump/Freund survey, students at University of Sheffield exhibited self-service behavior and responded, "Don't need to ask" when questioned about why they do not ask librarians for assistance (Bickley & Corrall, 2011, p. 233). Sheffield students prefer to ask "tutor/lecturer" or "other students" before seeking assistance from librarians and are similar to US students in that they do not have a clear understanding of librarianship in the academy, cannot differentiate library staff from librarians, do not know what tasks librarians perform or subject expertise they have, and are not aware of the educational requirements of librarians (Bickley & Corrall, 2011, pp. 234–235). These authors further suggest that comparisons with other libraries will allow "firmer conclusions to be drawn" (Bickley & Corrall, 2011, p. 240).

Two North Carolina libraries replicated the Online Computer Library Center (OCLC) 2005 *Perceptions of Libraries and Information Resources* global survey to investigate their students' perceptions about library services (Sutton, Bazirjian, & Zerwas, 2009, p. 474). This study compared survey results from libraries A and B and then assessed those findings against the conclusions drawn from the OCLC study. The authors of the North Carolina study conclude that the results reported in the OCLC study differ significantly from patrons' perspectives gathered at libraries A and B. Accordingly, Sutton et al. (2009) suggest that libraries should conduct studies locally and apply those findings to make informed changes in services or facilities (p. 484). The significant finding for libraries A and B was that students above all else selected the response "building/environment" when questioned about what brings them to the library, corroborating that library as place ranks high in students' perspectives. In other words, undergraduates are drawn to the more comfortable ambience of newly renovated spaces for private or group study.

In 2007, Oregon State University surveyed non-library users to find out why they were not using the physical or virtual library. After a major renovation of its Valley Library in 1999, the facility saw increased gate counts and high virtual resources usage but the researchers suspected that many students never visited the library. This project went outside the library to survey/interview students studying elsewhere to learn why they selected alternative sites for research and study (Vondracek, 2007, pp. 277–278). What the Valley Library staff found out again underlines the view that students want comfortable, quiet places to study, but the new IC and its "busyness" (Vondracek, 2007, p. 293) can be a deterrent and is distracting to some users. For these students virtual services appear to be in demand along with comfort and convenience. Vondracek (2007) speculates that relaxing library food and other restrictions might invite non-users back to the library (p. 292). This early view of the IC and the complexity of regulating collaborative and quiet zones persists in the University of Sheffield's study, indicating that services in the IC still require frequent review and adjustment to remain inviting spaces to students.

An early perception study conducted at Southern Illinois University verifies that many of the student perceptions about academic librarians have had a long life. This survey is based for the most part on an even earlier well documented questionnaire produced by Peter Heron and Maureen Pastine in 1977 (Fagan, 2003, p. 132). The Southern Illinois University library study expanded the three questions Heron and Pastine used to four, and queried students about their knowledge of a "librarian's education, skills, job, and personality" conjecturing that if students knew more about librarians they might be inclined to ask them for help (Fagan, 2003, p. 141). Fagan (2003) concludes that "as a group" students could not definitively say that knowing more about librarians would prompt them to seek help in the future (p. 141). However, she stresses the point made in the North Carolina study and in the anthropological studies that individual institutions should survey their students to discover the best approach for changing their perceptions about librarians in the library (Fagan, 2003, p. 141).

The Crump/Freund survey assessment validates many of the findings recorded in these studies and upholds the sentiment that library as place is alive and well on university campuses. However, librarians need to find a way to brand their services and expertise in order to remain a viable presence in the IC. To do that, we should invite students' questions and promote an ongoing dialogue between librarians and library users. Once we do that, librarians can set aside incorrect perceptions that may have steered library services on the wrong course.

The IC completely changed the way libraries interact with the patrons, re-established the library as place, and integrated technology in an effective way, but in the process disrupted the librarian's role. It is true that librarians have never been the most popular people on campus. Many authors have posited that historically librarians have reached only a small percentage of serious scholars in the academy. However, because these scholars had to come to the library to do their research and as reference librarians we were there to impart knowledge, we still felt integral to the research process. Now the students have unlimited resources found through discovery tools and, as the Crump/Freund survey confirms, preferably through Google. They are finding answers on their own and they seem to prefer it that way. We need to acknowledge that the students have moved on without us, they are producing, and they are graduating.

This may sound pessimistic but the authors are not. Librarians do not need to compete with Google; instead, we should strive to understand what makes Google work so well for the students and leverage that knowledge to create innovative services unique to the library. Library discovery services (such as Summon's OneSearch™ and EBSCO Discovery Service™) are a recent and encouraging development, but at the time of this publication, librarians have not fully embraced the concept. Is this a case once again of librarians' predilection for perfection getting in the way of timely development and implementation? In the introduction, the authors wrote about McRae's (2010) publication, *What Works*, and admired the overall optimism in the book. We found the "dare to be great" message inspiring. It gives the hope that through experimentation, innovation, and attracting creative staff, an institution can be successful. Through a far view planning approach, rather than the short-sighted view that every flaw in every venture must be fixed before it can be introduced, an institution might find a middle path that will encourage risk taking and allow it to be nimble and adaptable to change. Can a positive attitude pull librarians up and out of our funk? The authors think it can, but only if firmly grounded in a sense of community within the library and reaching out to the academy as a whole. As librarians we must constantly remind ourselves that the academy, the university community, *is* the students. They are our consumers and our advocates to the academic faculty members who too often ignore librarians as partners in the learning continuum. As McRae points out, "Communities mirror the frailties of humankind as well as its virtues. But as I have sought to argue, there is a collaborative sense too. It is a more complex community than it was a generation ago" (2010: 252). Within the academy, education is the focal point and reason for fostering community that attracts creativity and talented people who welcome the change we need to thrive.

Library mission should be the result of talking with library staff, academic faculty, and students or, more to the point, the whole community. It must be flexible and adaptable enough to last for a few years but should be reviewed regularly, tweaked when necessary, and shared with the community for input. The mission statement or strategic plan is a guide to the future but not a well-worn path. Communication of the library's mission to the community is the responsibility of the library staff and the administration alike. "Have a sense of mission: keep the long game in view and do right by those who share your objectives" (McRae, 2010: x).

What is preventing the formation of community in libraries? Munde and Marks delineate the significant divides between "stakeholder groups" and their perception of "what quality means in the library environment" (2009, p. 4). When assessment practices are put into place without communicating the purpose of the evaluation or a clear plan of action for use of the data, the resulting lack of buy-in from library staff assures that "measurement will be flawed and assessment is doomed" (Munde & Marks, 2010, p. 7). Michalko, Malpas, and Arcolio (2010) in their risk assessment of academic libraries, note the "conservative nature" of library organizations, warning about how it "inhibits timely adaption to changed circumstances" (p. 19). We acknowledge this warning and believe the risks identified in their analysis pinpoint the many obstacles that obstruct the way to building community. Pertinent to the Crump/Freund survey is the immediacy of their call for "collective effort and a new vision of services" and we share in the frustration that "incremental revision of traditional operational models" does not fully address or assert the true value of the library to the academic community (Michalko et al., 2010, p. 19). Yet the IC presents new opportunities for reaching out to customers and building a user-based community that advances "a culture that encourages innovation and flexibility beyond a traditional hierarchical culture" (Nunn & Ruane, 2011, p. 294).

As a profession we want to remain relevant within the research community. How do we begin? We begin with us. If we want to regain relevancy, librarians need to stop making assumptions about customers by engaging with them to keep pace with their evolving needs. The Crump/Freund survey shows that across all participating libraries, the students have a generally favorable view of librarians and library staff, although there are clearly some indications in the open remarks that students have had isolated unfavorable encounters. We need to acknowledge that our approach as an expert may discourage more than it encourages. The current generation of technically savvy and time-challenged students want convenience, transparency, and discoverability, putting them squarely in command of the process. They do not want to dig for information; they are surfers and have been since grade school. This is difficult for librarians who aspire to show the patrons the right way to do research while knowing full well that students are in a hurry, in a constant state of multi-tasking, and impatient with long explanations. When they do decide to consult with a librarian, we need to be sure that our customers get an answer or they may leave in discouragement and not come back. Librarians should practice humility in success and failure, as McRae (2010: x) advises, and consider if the need to provide a teachable moment is the best way to approach every interaction with the customer.

In his remarks at the plenary session of the 2008 Reference Renaissance: Current and Future Trends conference, David Lankes, said "Why do we think our job is to get someone to a resource and not to an answer?" (2010: 18–19). He spoke of the user or "member" and questioned whether he/she is really ever in control of the reference transaction. This is exactly how the library staff needs to think of the patron, as a "member" of the library community who has a say in how the service transaction progresses. Lankes goes on to say that "as librarians we must always remember that the member is learning about his or her topic, not the nuances of librarianship and search strategy" (2010, p. 19). Marie Radford (2011) raises a similar point, citing her studies that have indicated that as much as one-third of all chat transactions end abruptly. Her researchers looked over chat transcripts and found evidence that the librarian's pointed questions (for example, "what databases have you used?") result in an immediate end to the transaction, an indication that perhaps the student was embarrassed to say they had not started or had perhaps started in the wrong database.

From the Crump/Freund survey we know students do not trust the librarians' advice nor do they consider us at all. However, other studies have demonstrated that users and librarians share frustration with library databases and search engines. Why not begin the research interview at that level, putting ourselves in the customer's place? They may have not found the "best" resource, but does it really matter? We are not sure it should. Librarians have long been hung up on the precept that knowledge is good or bad, right or wrong – we need to relax the authority role, practice a softer touch to truly connect with students in a more humane manner, as collaborator and colleague in the academy. This is what LaBaugh (2008) and Maxfield before him were talking about – the "counselor" or "therapist" librarian concept discussed in Chapter 2. Rather than correcting the client who comes to the librarian for help, accept that person's presentation of the issue and do something about it. LaBaugh states that if a patron cannot find a book on the shelf, it is "not a problem with their cognitive ability, rather it is our problem." (2008: 42) This is the kind of helpful service philosophy we all cherish.

The focus is the patron. In the framework of the information and learning commons, librarians envisioned a collaborative research environment where they could serve students; however, that model turned out to be the same reference desk prettied up with a new shade of lipstick. We need to step away from the old model and connect with our patrons as partners in developing services that respond to their learning habits and schedules. By involving users in conversations that will help us understand their research perspective, we will discover true customer concerns rather than characterizing users' needs based on librarians' assumptions and work routines. Can we close the gap and promote services that work for the whole community? We can, if we are willing to ask the questions:

- Have you determined when most students are in the building? Should library staff, including the professional librarians, adopt more flexible work schedules to be available when customers really need them?

- When is the last time you asked students how they like your library services? How often do you engage with students in some way; not only through surveys but in face-to-face discussions and spontaneous conversations (for example, "did I answer your question today?").

- Have you collaborated with students or teaching faculty in the planning process for a service or building project? In a library grant?

- When your library has tried a new service – such as chat, Facebook, a mobile information cart – does everyone get involved or is it usually an initiative of one or two librarians? Does everyone help market new services?

- Mobility is one way to be available 24/7 anytime, anywhere. Is this realistic for your library and a service your customers would use?

- Nearly everyone has a cellphone. Is your information and/or reference line posted for all to see? What do you need to do to make the library's existing phone service known and ubiquitous?

- Do students want to see embedded librarians where they are working such as in online courses or in course management systems or on interlibrary loan/course reserves system pages? If they do, how can you enlist their help to get the teaching faculty interested?

- There is some mounting evidence that departmental and small branch libraries may be on the chopping block due to budget constraints and there is a corresponding move toward large information commons and combined library facilities. Do students like the "big box" library? Are they getting service or disservice?

- Or do customers prefer departmental libraries that cater to specific disciplines?

- Or do customers want librarians embedded in their college department? Their dorms? The student union?

- What if they want it all? How will you involve library staff and the whole university community in determining priority services?

Too many questions? The answers are not that difficult if we talk, experiment, act, embrace the customer's world, leave our world behind, and walk across the divide.

References

Bickley, R., & Corrall, S. (2011). Student perceptions of staff in the Information Commons: A survey at the University of Sheffield. *Reference Services Review*, *39*(2), 223–243. DOI: 10.1108/00907321111135466

Fagan, J. (2003). Students' perceptions of academic librarians. *The Reference Librarian*, *37*(78), 131–148. DOI: 10.1300/J120v37n78_09

Kennedy, S. (2011). Farewell to the reference librarian. *Journal of Library Administration*, *51*(4), 319–325. DOI: 10.1080/01930826.2011.556954

LaBaugh, R. T. (2008) Solution focused reference: Counselor librarianship revisited. In M. L. Madden & S. K. Steiner (Eds.), *The desk and beyond: Next generation reference services* (pp. 38–52). Chicago, IL: Association of College and Research Libraries.

Lankes, D. R. (2010). Theory meets practice: Educators and directors talk (plenary panel). In Radford, M. L. & Lankes, D. R. (Eds.), *Reference renaissance: Current and future trends* (pp. 17–20). New York, NY: Neal-Schuman Publishers.

McRae, H. (2010). *What works: Success in stressful times*. London: Harper Press.

Michalko, J., Malpas, C., & Arcolio, A. (2010). *Research libraries, risks and systemic change*. Dublin, OH: OCLC Research. Retrieved from *http://www.oclc.org/research/publications/library/2010/2010-03.pdf*

Munde, G., & Marks, K. (2009). *Surviving the future: Academic libraries, quality, and assessment*. Oxford: Chandos.

Nunn, B., & Ruane, E. (2011). Marketing gets personal: Promoting reference staff to reach users. *Journal of Library Administration*, *51*(3), 291–300. DOI: 10.1080/01930826.2011.556945

O'Connor, F. (1979). *Mystery and manners; Occasional prose, selected & edited by Sally and Robert Fitzgerald*. New York: Farrar, Straus & Giroux.

Radford, M. L. (2011, March). A future in transition: Foreseeing forthcoming opportunities & challenges in academic reference [preview webcast for the Association of College and Research Libraries (ACRL) 2011 Virtual Conference, Philadelphia, PA]. Retrieved from *http://www.acrl.ala.org/acrlinsider/archives/3192*

Sutton, L., Bazirjian, R., & Zerwas, S. (2009). Library service perceptions: A study of two universities. *College & Research Libraries*, *70*(5), 474–495. Retrieved from *http://crl.acrl.org/content/70/5/474.full.pdf+html*

Vondracek, R. (2007). Comfort and convenience? Why students choose alternatives to the library. *portal: Libraries and the Academy*, 7(3), 277–293. Retrieved from *http://muse.jhu.edu/journals/portal_libraries_and_the_academy/v007/7.3vondracek.html*

Appendix A: Library user survey

Informed Consent

Protocol Title: Meeting the Needs of Student Users in Academic Libraries

Please read this consent document carefully before you decide to participate in this study.

Purpose of the research study: This study is designed to determine if the learning spaces and services provided by academic libraries are functioning as intended. It will also investigate the divergence of perceptions between academic library users and academic library staff.

What you will be asked to do in the study: You will be asked to complete a survey responding as accurately as possible based on your experience with and perceptions of the library facility and services. These questions will include some very basic demographic information as well as your purpose in using the library today.

Time required: Completion of the survey should take roughly 10–15 minutes.

Risks and Benefits: No risk is anticipated for the participant with completing the survey. You will not directly benefit from participation.

Compensation: There is no direct compensation for participating in this research.

Confidentiality: Your identity will be kept confidential to the extent provided by law. Your survey answers will be collected with no identification of individual respondents. When the study is completed and the captured data is analyzed, the data will be destroyed and your information will be kept confidential. You will not be required to state your name in any part of the testing.

Voluntary participation: Your participation in this study is completely voluntary.

Right to withdraw from the study: You have the right to withdraw from the study at any time without consequence. You may skip questions or stop participating at any time.

Who to contact if you have questions about the study: Michele Crump, George A. Smathers Libraries, UF, PO Box 117025, Gainesville, FL 32611, mcrump@ufl.edu / 352.273.2717, or LeiLani Freund, George A. Smathers Libraries, UF, PO Box 117022, Gainesville, FL 32611, leilanif@ufl.edu / 352.273.2622.

Who to contact about your rights as a research participant in the study: IRB02 Office, Box 112250, University of Florida, Gainesville, FL 326112250 / 352.392.0433.

Agreement

*1. I have read the procedure described above. I voluntarily agree to participate in the survey and I have received a copy of this description.

○ Yes

○ No

2. Why do you usually come into the library? (Select up to 3)

☐ Need a comfortable, quiet place to study

☐ Check my email

☐ Collaborate with others on a project

☐ Use a computer workstation for a class assignment

☐ Use a computer workstation for personal/social activities (Facebook, Twitter, Web browsing, job searching, gaming, etc.)

☐ Use a copier or scanner

☐ Check-out or renew books

☐ Check on status of overdue fines or lost items

☐ Browse the collection

☐ Use course reserves

☐ Use interlibrary loan

☐ Consult with a librarian about a class assignment or group project

☐ Consult with a librarian about my thesis or dissertation

☐ Get a study or media room for my group

---

* Questions marked with an asterisk must be answered. If the participant responds "no" to Q1, they are taken out of the survey.

☐ Watch a video/DVD

☐ Check-out a laptop or other equipment

☐ Get coffee/snacks and/or hang out with friends

☐ Take a class or workshop on library resources

☐ I don't come to the library.

☐ Other (please specify)

*3. Do you ever use library services or resources from outside the library?

○ Yes

○ No

Use From Outside Library

4. When not in the library, how do you access services or resources? (Select all that apply)

☐ From home/dorm computer

☐ From phone

☐ From laptop, tablet (iPad), netbook

5. What services or resources do you use from outside the library? (Select all that apply)

☐ Chat / IM / Ask a Librarian services

☐ Course reserves

☐ Interlibrary loan requests

☐ Delivery from storage or closed stacks

☐ Phone calls to the reference or circulation desk

☐ Phone calls to specific librarian (someone you know or have worked with before)

☐ Text message to a librarian

☐ Library or librarian Facebook site

☐ Library or librarian Twitter site

☐ Library or librarian blog

☐ Library online

☐ Catalog

☐ Library databases

☐ Library "how to get started" Web pages

☐ Library online circulation services (renewals, holds, etc.)

☐ Other (please specify)

Does Not Access Library from Outside

6. Why don't you use library services or resources from outside the library?

○ I prefer to go to the library

○ I don't know what number to call when I have a question

○ I have never figured out how to get to ebooks, ejournals or library services from home

○ I can't find what I need on the library Web pages

○ Other (please specify)

7. When you have a paper to write, how do you start your research? (Select up to 3 starting points)

☐ Google

☐ Google Scholar

☐ Wikipedia

☐ At the library home page

☐ At the library catalog

☐ Online library tutorials

☐ "How to get started" Web pages

☐ Library FAQ

☐ Library subject guides

☐ Reference books or encyclopedias

☐ I browse the library book shelves

☐ I ask a librarian for help

☐ I ask my instructor or use course materials

☐ I ask my classmates

☐ I ask my parents

☐ Other (please specify)

8. When you come to the library, do you ever ask library staff for help with your research, for a class assignment, etc.?

○ Yes, often

○ Yes, occasionally

○ Never (if never, please explain why not)

9. When you have a library reference or service question, how do you prefer to contact the library? (Select up to 3 preferences)

☐ Inperson service at public desks

☐ Office consultations

☐ Chat/IM

☐ Phone (Voice)

☐ Phone (Text)

☐ Email

☐ Facebook

☐ Twitter

☐ Blogs

☐ N/A – I never contact the library

☐ Other (please specify)

10. In general, how do you perceive library staff? (Select up to 3)

☐ Generally helpful

☐ Rule enforcer/monitor

☐ Too much information

☐ Advisor/consultant

☐ Helpful for technical problems

☐ Helpful for research problems

☐ Instructor – they show me how to find what I need or want

☐ Content provider – they get me what I need or want

☐ Irrelevant – I can find all I need online without a librarian's help

☐ Internet/technology expert

☐ N/A – I never interact with library staff

☐ Other (please describe)

11. What do you think of the present library facility?

	Yes	No
Are service desks well located?	O	O
Is there adequate furniture?	O	O
Is there adequate space?	O	O
Is there adequate space for collaborative/group study?	O	O
Is there adequate space for individual study?	O	O
Is there adequate equipment?	O	O
Is the library adequately staffed?	O	O
Is the library safe and secure?	O	O
Is the library clean and inviting?	O	O

Please explain any "No" answers and describe any other issues.

*12. What is your status?

O Undergraduate
O Graduate
O Post-Bac
O Full-time faculty
O Part-time faculty
O Visitor
O University staff
O University alumni

Undergraduate and Graduate

13. What is your discipline or area of study? (Please indicate if you have not declared a major.)

Faculty and Staff

14. What is your department?

[ ]

Visitors

15. What is your affiliation?

O Unaffilated
O University affiliation, please explain.

[ ]

Alumni

16. What is the year of your graduation or final degree?

[ ]

Residence

17. Is your residence:

O On-campus
O Off-campus

Thank you

Thank you for taking our survey.

Appendix B: Library staff survey

Informed Consent

Protocol Title: Meeting the Needs of Student Users in Academic Libraries

Please read this consent document carefully before you decide to participate in this study.

Purpose of the research study: This study is designed to determine if the learning spaces and services provided by academic libraries are functioning as intended. It will also investigate the divergence of perceptions between academic library users and academic library staff.

What you will be asked to do in the study: You will be asked to complete a survey responding as accurately as possible based on your experience with and perceptions of the library facility and services and how the students use them. These questions will include some very basic demographic information as well as your specific public service duties.

Time required: Completion of the survey should take roughly 15 minutes.

Risks and Benefits: No risk is anticipated for the participant with completing the survey. You will not directly benefit from participation.

Compensation: There is no direct compensation for participating in this research.

Confidentiality: Your identity will be kept confidential to the extent provided by law. Your survey answers will be collected with no identification of individual respondents. When the study is completed and the captured data is analyzed, the data will be destroyed and your information will be kept confidential. You will not be required to state your name in any part of the testing.

Voluntary participation: Your participation in this study is completely voluntary.

Right to withdraw from the study: You have the right to withdraw from the study at any time without consequence. You may skip questions or stop participating at any time.

Who to contact if you have questions about the study: Michele Crump, George A. Smathers Libraries, UF, PO Box 117025, Gainesville, FL 32611 / mcrump@ufl.edu / 352.273.2717, or LeiLani Freund, George A. Smathers Libraries, UF, PO Box 117022, Gainesville, FL 32611 leilanif@ufl.edu / 352.273.2622.

Who to contact about your rights as a research participant in the study: IRB02 Office, Box 112250, University of Florida, Gainesville, FL 326112250 / 352.392.0433.

Agreement

*1. I have read the procedure described above. I voluntarily agree to participate in the survey and I have received a copy of this description.
O Yes
O No

2. In your current library position, where do you serve the library patrons? (Select all that apply to your job duties)
□ Information desk
□ Reference or research desk
□ Circulation desk
□ Interlibrary Loan office or desk
□ Course Reserves office or desk
□ Technical support desk
□ Combined desk
□ Classroom (bibliographic instruction)
□ Online (virtual or chat reference; email reference)
□ Office consultations
□ Phone (voice)
□ Phone (texting)
□ Other (please describe)

* Questions marked with an asterisk must be answered. If the participant responds "no" to Q1, they are taken out of the survey. For Q3 and Q12, the participant is directed to further questions depending on their answer.

3. **How do you serve the patron? (Select up to 3 functions you most perform)**

☐ Directional assistance

☐ Check-out or renew materials

☐ Interlibrary Loan services

☐ Course Reserves services

☐ Computer (hardware and software) assistance

☐ Assistance with copiers, scanners, or printers

☐ Refer patron to other library services

☐ Check-out a study or media room

☐ Answer reference questions

☐ Help students with class assignments

☐ Consultations with undergraduates and graduate students

☐ Check-out laptop or other equipment

☐ Check status of overdue fines or lost items

☐ Other (please specify)

4. **Why do you think most students come into the library? (Select up to 3)**

☐ Comfortable, quiet place to study

☐ Check email

☐ Collaborate with others on a project

☐ Use a computer workstation for a class assignment

☐ Use a computer workstation for personal/social activities (Facebook, Twitter, Web browsing, job searching, gaming, etc.)

☐ Use a copier or scanner

☐ Check-out or renew books

☐ Check on status of overdue fines or lost items

☐ Browse the collection

☐ Use course reserves

☐ Use interlibrary loan

☐ Consult with librarian about a class assignment or group project

☐ Consult with librarian about thesis or dissertation

☐ Get a study or media room for a group

☐ Watch a video/DVD

☐ Check-out a laptop or other equipment

☐ Get coffee/snacks and/or hang out with friends

☐ Take a class or workshop on library resources

☐ Other (please specify)

5. My library offers the following assistance: (Select all that apply)

☐ In-person service at public desks

☐ Consultations with librarians/subject specialists

☐ Chat or IM services

☐ Phone reference service

☐ Email reference service

☐ Text messaging service

☐ Library Facebook site

☐ Individual librarian Facebook sites

☐ Library Twitter sites

☐ Individual librarian Twitter sites

☐ Library blogs

☐ Individual librarian blogs

☐ Other (please specify)

6. When I perform Reference services I prefer the following: (Please rank in preference, 1 = most preferred to 9 = least preferred)

	1	2	3	4	5	6	7	8	9
In-person service at public desks	O	O	O	O	O	O	O	O	O
Office consultations	O	O	O	O	O	O	O	O	O
Chat/IM	O	O	O	O	O	O	O	O	O
Phone (voice)	O	O	O	O	O	O	O	O	O
Phone (text)	O	O	O	O	O	O	O	O	O
Email	O	O	O	O	O	O	O	O	O
Facebook	O	O	O	O	O	O	O	O	O
Twitter	O	O	O	O	O	O	O	O	O
Blogs	O	O	O	O	O	O	O	O	O

Comments

7. When resources are scarce, what Reference Services do you think should be offered? (Please rank in preference, 1 = most preferred to 9 = least preferred)

	1	2	3	4	5	6	7	8	9
In-person service at public desks	O	O	O	O	O	O	O	O	O
Office consultations	O	O	O	O	O	O	O	O	O
Chat/IM	O	O	O	O	O	O	O	O	O
Phone (voice)	O	O	O	O	O	O	O	O	O
Phone (text)	O	O	O	O	O	O	O	O	O
Email	O	O	O	O	O	O	O	O	O
Facebook	O	O	O	O	O	O	O	O	O
Twitter	O	O	O	O	O	O	O	O	O
Blogs	O	O	O	O	O	O	O	O	O

Other (please specify)

8. When you advise a patron on how to start their research, where do you begin most frequently? (Select up to 3 starting points)

☐ Google

☐ Google Scholar

☐ Wikipedia

☐ At the library home page

☐ At the library catalog

☐ Reference interview

☐ Online Library tutorials

☐ How to get started Web pages

☐ Library FAQ

☐ Library subject guides

☐ Reference books or encyclopedias

☐ Give them a call number section to browse

☐ Suggest an appointment with a subject specialist librarian

☐ Other (please specify)

9. How do you think most patrons perceive library staff in your institution? (Select up to 3)

☐ Generally helpful

☐ Rule enforcer/monitor

☐ Too much information

☐ Advisor/consultant

☐ Helpful for technical problems

☐ Helpful for research problems

☐ Instructor – showing them how to find what they need or want

☐ Content provider – getting them what they need or want

☐ Irrelevant – patrons feel they can find all they need online

☐ Internet/technology expert

Other (please specify)

10. Please describe your present facility.

	Yes	No
Are service desks well located?	O	O
Is there adequate furniture?	O	O
Is there adequate space?	O	O
Is there adequate space for collaborative/group study?	O	O
Is there adequate space for individual study?	O	O
Is there adequate equipment?	O	O
Is the library adequately staffed?	O	O
Is the library safe and secure?	O	O
Is the library clean and inviting?	O	O

Please explain any "No" answers and describe any other issues.

11. Has your library undergone a large renovation or added/remodeled space (e.g. Information Commons) in the past 5 years?

O Yes

O No

O I don't know

12. Is your library a new building and was it built in the past 5 years?

○ Yes

○ No

○ I don't know

13. Please rate the following building features in your library:

	Poor	Below Average	Satisfactory	Above Average	Excellent
General layout/ building design	○	○	○	○	○
Lighting	○	○	○	○	○
Materials (floors, paint, etc.)	○	○	○	○	○
Overall environment	○	○	○	○	○
Book/Bound Serials stacks	○	○	○	○	○
Information Commons	○	○	○	○	○
Study space	○	○	○	○	○
Circulation/Info Desks	○	○	○	○	○
Reference Desk	○	○	○	○	○
Staff Offices	○	○	○	○	○
Staff Meeting Rooms	○	○	○	○	○
Elevators	○	○	○	○	○
Work areas/ Office layout	○	○	○	○	○

Professional Background Information

14. What is your position?

○ Student employee

○ Temporary staff

○ Permanent staff

○ Librarian

○ Administrative

15. How many years have you been in your present position?

○ 0–2 years
○ 3–5 years
○ 6–10 years
○ 11–20 years
○ 21 or more years

16. How many years have you been in the library profession?
○ 0–2 years
○ 3–5 years
○ 6–10 years
○ 11–20 years
○ 21 or more years

Library User Engagement Information

17. Does your library conduct usability testing?

○ Yes

○ No
○ I don't know

If yes, please describe what kind of testing and how often testing is done.

18. Does your library conduct user surveys?

○ Yes

○ No

○ I don't know

If yes, please describe how often user surveys are conducted.

19. Does your library conduct focus group discussions and interviews with users?

○ Yes

○ No

○ I don't know

If yes, please describe how often focus group discussions are conducted.

Thank you

Thank you for taking our survey.

Index

CPSIA information can be obtained at www.ICGtesting.com
Printed in the USA
LVOW01s1459070115

421885LV00005B/93/P